LEWIS MORRIS

Anglo-American Statesman

LEWIS MORRIS

Anglo-American Statesman

ca. 1613–1691

by

Samuel Stelle Smith

First published in 1983 in the United States of America by Humanities Press Inc., Atlantic Highlands, NJ 07716

E
191
M67
S54
1983

©Copyright 1983 by Samuel Stelle Smith

Library of Congress Cataloging in Publication Data

Smith, Samuel Stelle.
  Lewis Morris, Anglo-American statesman, ca. 1613-1691.

  Bibliography: p.
  1. Morris, Lewis, ca. 1613-1691.   2. Statesmen—United States—Biography.   I. Title.
E191.M67S54   1983   973.2′092′4 [B]   82-15381
ISBN 0-391-02767-0

MANUFACTURED IN THE UNITED STATES OF AMERICA

To my wife

Agnes

TABLE OF CONTENTS

PLATES

PLATE 1
Based on map *Insulae Americanae in Oceano Septentrionali cum Terris adiacentibus*. This map appears in a 1635 atlas published by Wilhelm and Johannem Blaeu. Atlas in The Library of Congress. The Blaeu map was used mainly to verify 17th century place names.

PLATE 2
Based on map *A topographicall Description and Admeasurement of the Yland of Barbados in the West Indyaes with the Mrs Names of the Severall plantacons*. This map was published in 1657 as an insert in "A True and Exact History of the Island of Barbados," by Richard Ligon. The map was probably executed in 1647–50 while Ligon was in Barbados. Copies are in The Library of Congress, Yale University Library and New York Public Library. The location of forts shown on this map and described in Chapter 7, are based on map *A New Map of The Island of Barbados*, by Philip Lea in the New York Public Library, ascribed to 1690.

PLATE 3
Based on map *The Islands of Scilly*, by T. Kitchen, in New York Public Library and ascribed to 1753. Also consulted was the 1670 map of Scilly Islands in The Library of Congress, "Hydrographia Universalis," by Philip Lea.

PLATE 4
Based on map *De Manatus op de Noort Riuier*. The original of this 1639 map has been lost. Two copies, made between 1665 and 1670, are in existence. The Harrisse copy by John Vingboons, made for the West Indies Company of Holland, is in The Library of Congress. The Costello copy is in the Medici Library, Florence, Italy. A copy of the Costello copy is in "The Iconography of Manhattan Island 1498–1909," by I.N.P. Stokes, published in 1918.

PLATE 5

Based on map *Assbeeldinge van de Stadt Amsterdam in Nieuw Neederlandt* and known street locations of the Steenwyck and Morris houses. This 1660 map is in the Medici Library, Florence, Italy. The Library of Congress has a glass negative of the map. A copy is in the "Iconography of Manhattan Island 1498–1909," by I.N.P. Stokes, published in 1918.

PLATE 6

Section of figurative map in The British Museum titled *Pennsylvania Nio Caesaria Vulgo New Jersey*, ascribed to 1682 or 1683. At this point in time, Sandy Hook was attached to the Highlands of Navesink, then called "Portland." The Navesink River shown under Portland ran directly out to sea over what is now the Sea Bright strip. Passage Point, now the end of Rumson peninsula, is shown just upland of what is labeled "Sandy Land." "Collonel Morris his Iron Works" is shown in the upper reaches of the Navesink River. A facsimile of photograph of the original is in the Crown Collection of American Maps selected by Archer Butler Hulbert.

PLATE 7

Map of Shrewsbury town lots prepared from deed research by James Steen and Samuel S. Smith. Map includes entire present boro of Shrewsbury and parts of Red Bank, Little Silver, Oceanport, Eaton-town and Tinton Falls. Modern road designations are used. Additional details on town lots appear on a 1963 version of this map published in "Sandy Hook and the Land of the Navesink," by Samuel Stelle Smith.

Preface

Colonel Lewis Morris has been one of the most overlooked shapers of early colonial American history. There never has been a biography written about him nor is he mentioned in major biographical dictionaries. Yet, he was one of the most influential and colorful men in middle and late 17th century American public affairs.

In the nearly 300 years since his death in 1691, the accomplishments of Colonel Lewis Morris have remained mostly hidden, partly because he destroyed many of his papers before his death and partly because of the confusion brought about by the fact that there were three Lewis Morrises living in the same house during the same period, all three of whom rose to high positions in colonial New York and New Jersey government.

For purposes of identification, the author has labeled these three: Colonel Lewis Morris, Governor Lewis Morris and Lewis Morris of Passage Point. Governor Lewis Morris was the son of Colonel Lewis Morris' younger brother, Richard Morris—the son becoming the Colonel's ward at age one upon the sudden death of his mother and father. Lewis Morris of Passage Point was the son of a "relation," Thomas Morris of Barbados—this child also becoming the ward of the Colonel in "infancy."

Colonel Lewis Morris began his career in 1629, at about age 16, as an apprentice navigator for The Providence Island Company, a British colonizing and privateering venture in the Caribbean that sometimes turned to piracy for which Morris was twice imprisoned. Morris remained with The Providence Island Company for about 15 years and rose to become one of the principals in the company's Caribbean operations.

In 1646 or 1647 at about age 33, having acquired considerable wealth with The Providence Island Company, Lewis Morris retired from the sea and became a shipping merchant and plantation owner in Barbados, dealing mostly in sugar and rum. During the next 20 years, Morris studied law, and in addition to carrying on his mercantile business, he rose to become a member of the Governing Council of Barbados. It was during this period that Morris actively supported Oliver Cromwell's parliamentary cause in Barbados and elsewhere for which Cromwell made Morris a colonel.

In 1664, when the British took New York from the Dutch, Colonel Morris came to America where he continued his shipping business and also entered politics.

The Colonel was soon on the governing council of both New York and East New Jersey and the head of the East New Jersey Court of Common Right, which was the supreme court of the province. During his many years of service in these newly formed provinces, he brought to these governments many judicial and legislative innovations, some of them with a distinct Barbadian flavor.

To his ward Lewis Morris of Passage Point the Colonel gave a plantation in Monmouth County and arranged for him to become the first High Sheriff of Monmouth County. To his ward Governor Lewis Morris he taught the law, whereupon at age 21, he was placed on the Governing Council of East New Jersey—later becoming Chief Justice of New York and finally the first Royal Governor of New Jersey.

Governor Lewis Morris became the father of a Lewis Morris who was on the Governing Council of New York and whose son Lewis Morris became a signer of the Declaration of Independence and another son, Gouverneur Morris who became the writer of the final draft of the Constitution of the United States.

Although Colonel Lewis Morris had no known children of his own, his two wards left 22 children and over 100 grandchildren between them, many of whom down through the generations carried on the Morris inclination to statesmanship. All of them do not bear the name of Morris but they are Morrises none the less. For example, Governor Thomas Kean, present governor of New Jersey is a Morris—so are Richard Nixon and Jimmy Carter, recent Presidents of the United States, as revealed in the appendix genealogy of the book.

1

Apprentice Navigator

In his nearly eighty years, from circa 1613 to 1691, Lewis Morris lived what might be called two lives. To some of his contemporaries, he was a respected churchman, planter, merchant, lawyer, statesman and chief justice of the supreme court, enjoying the confidence of royal governors and kings. To others, he was a daring pirate and privateer, plundering from port to port, killing when his way was blocked—a man who was twice thrown into prison, where he spent long confinements in chains.

These two lives of Lewis Morris, although appearing to set up a paradox, were basically not inconsistent. Lewis Morris was not a man who was one character one moment, and another man at the next. Fate did help his essential drive to carry him along varied paths, but, over each, he was quite consistent—a man full of energy, ambition and talent, who seemed to approach every challenge of life as though it were his last.

Before his death, Lewis Morris destroyed all of his personal papers and records, giving rise to a suspicion that in the end he was dissatisfied with the course of his life, and wished to have it buried.

To help Lewis Morris bury his past, or at least help obscure it from future historians, was the fact that there were two additional Lewis Morrises who flourished at the same time in the same area that he did. One was Lewis, son of Thomas Morris, and the other was Lewis, son of Richard Morris. To add to the confusion, all three Lewis Morrises, at sometime in the course of their lives, were called Colonel Lewis Morris.

Nothing that can be reliably documented, is known of the family background of the subject Lewis Morris.[1] Further, nothing is known of him, personally, until 1629, when at about age 16, he became an indentured servant and member of a ship's company bound for the Caribbean to help the Earl of Warwick establish a new island colony for Britain.[2] That same year, Warwick helped organize the Massachusetts Bay Colony under Governor John Winthrop. Previously, Warwick had been instrumental in the 1609 Virginia settlement. This time he was directing his attentions to a small island off the "Moskito Coast" of Nicaragua, Central America. Spain called the island Santa Catalina, which Britain would rename Providence Island.[3]

Captain Dan Elfrith was designated to be Governor of the Providence Island settlement. Elfrith had a long and daring record as a privateer against Spain, much of it in the very waters to which he was returning. Some of his privateering ventures had been in association with the Earl of Warwick. One joint venture resulted in supplying the first slaves brought to the American colonies in 1619. Elfrith had plundered a Spanish slave ship and sold half the slaves in Virginia and the other half in Bermuda, in the name of the Earl of Warwick.[4]

Officially the voyage to Providence Island was one of colonization. Probably a majority of the 20 Warwick Puritan associates in the enterprise believed the settlement to be only for that purpose. There is reliable evidence, however, that some of the sponsors were aware from the start that the settlement might also become a privateering base against Spanish shipping in the Caribbean. A clear sign of the aggressive nature of the venture, in addition to the past records of some of its participants such as Captain Elfrith's, was the granting of letters of marque to the colonizers a month before they left England.[5]

As to privateering, Britain was at war with Spain, and Britain could not support the conflict with government funds alone, thus the government sponsored privateering by issuing letters of marque, with four-fifths of the prize to go to the adventurers. In this way, Britain could not only wage war with Spain, but she could colonize in the same theatre of operation.

Three ships were fitted out for the voyage to Providence Island. They were the *Warwick* of eighty tons burden, the *Somers Island* of one hundred tons, and the *Robert* of fifty tons. Young Lewis Morris was indentured for three years as apprentice navigator with the fleet of three ships.[6]

The Providence Island colonists set sail from England the second week in October 1629. Bermuda was to be the first port of call. During this early period, Bermuda was the principal British island colony in the western world, although it had been settled only since 1612.

Other British island settlements in the west, at this time, were limited to Barbados and St. Christopher, now St. Kitts. Barbados had been settled by Britain with a small group at Holetown in 1627, and with another at Bridgetown in 1628. St. Christopher had been settled by British adventurers in 1623. Two years later, in 1625, the French put a settlement there. By 1627 the British and French agreed to divide the island, but in 1629, shortly before the departure of the Providence Island settlers from England, a Spanish fleet fell upon both the British and French colonies and drove them off the island.

This was typical of the fluid situation in the Caribbean in 1629. The French and British (as well as the Dutch) held some territory, but the Spanish had long controlled most of the Caribbean Islands, plus the coast line of the mainland encompassing the Caribbean.

The Providence Island colonists made the Atlantic crossing to Bermuda on schedule, but on arrival there, problems soon developed. There were to be no women in the group of settlers, which caused considerable difficulty and delay in their recruiting efforts at Bermuda. When at length, the needed settlers were recruited, the three ships set sail for Providence Island, stopping first at San Andreas or San Andres Island, called Henrietta by the British, lying to the southwest of Providence. The colonists arrived at Providence about Christmas day 1629.

News of the departure from England of the Providence Island settlement was ultimately circulated in London. The diarist, John Rous, recorded that there was an island twenty miles long and ten miles broad (actually six long and four broad) which had been discovered by one of the Earl of Warwick's sea captains, and a group of settlers were already enroute.

Not long thereafter, Warwick confirmed the rumor by announcing the organization of a company with the formidable title: *The Governor and Company of Adventurers of the City of Westminster for the Plantation of the Island of Providence and Henrietta and the Adjacent Islands Lying Upon the Coast of America.* [7]

Upon the arrival of the three ships at Providence, the members of the colony immediately set about choosing plots of ground. Next, they started to clear the tillable land preparatory to planting crops. Lewis Morris was not a member of the farming segment of the colony. He was a part of the ship's company, which soon was sent off in relays to Nicaragua and coastal islands to trade with the native Indians. This was part of the planned purpose of the settlement. Of course they must always be on the alert. To be seen by the Spaniards meant that they would be attacked. Spain made great wealth from her trade with the Indians, and she meant to protect that trade.

Tobacco was to be the principal crop of the farming segment of the Providence Island colony, although this was distasteful to some of the Puritan sponsors of the settlement who disapproved of smoking. By August, a crop had been raised and it appeared to be of fine quality, but these encouraging signs were soon to fade. Something prevented the proper maturing of the crop after it was harvested, and it turned out to be of little value. This was the beginning of disaster for the colony, in which young Lewis Morris was to share a major responsibility.

1. *The History of Monmouthshire* by Joseph A. Bradney (1907–1932) states that Lewis Morris was of Tintern Parva, near Tintern Abbey, Monmouthshire, Wales, and that he resided there for much of his early life. Bradney also states that Lewis Morris was the brother of William Morris whose grandson, Valentine Morris, was of that place. An exchange of letters in 1762 and 1763 between the same Valentine Morris and Robert Hunter Morris, great-nephew of Lewis Morris, subject of this biography, could establish no relationship between these two Morris families, even at such an early date. (Morris: VM Nov. 8, 1762/RHM June 7, 1763) Further, at the death of Richard Morris, a known brother of the subject Lewis Morris, Richard was referred to in a letter of condolence to Lewis Morris as follows, "you have lost an only brother so have I a dear friend." (St. 4:15)

2. Camden 3:34; Newton 51–54. There is no record of Lewis Morris' first employment in this colonizing venture but there is a record of his leaving the colony in 1631. (See Ch. II, note 1.)

3. The island is now called Old Providence to distinguish it from New Providence in the Bahama group of islands.

4. Manchester Papers 261: Jan. 20, 1619/20; ibid 275: Oct. 9, 1620.

5. PRO Register book of Letters of Marque 1629.

6. CO Col. Entry Bk. Vol. III, p.103–107; CSPC 1574–1660:166.

7. CO Col. Entry Bk. Vol. IV p.1–10; CSPC 1574–1660:123.

2

Caribbean Pirate

The first sign of real trouble in the colony was when Captain Dan Elfrith and Captain Sam Axe, governor and deputy governor of the settlement, quarreled over their respective shares in the almost valueless tobacco crop. The breach between these two leaders soon grew wider, and before the end of 1631, Captain Axe with a few others, among them Lewis Morris, left Providence Island for one of the larger Moskito Cays, just off the coast of Nicaragua.

Lewis Morris is said to have severed his connection with the Providence Island settlement at this time. But according to the Providence Island Company "Minute Book" he was "discharged from the Company service."[1]

The following may have had some bearing on Morris' discharge. Shortly after the settlers arrived on Providence, some of the men deliberately set about plundering Spanish ships, even though there had been a peace with Spain proclaimed in November 1630, and the colonists had been so informed. Technically, Britain now being at peace with Spain, these plundering activities became piracy.

Captain Axe and his followers argued that the mere signing of a peace treaty 7,000 miles away was not applicable to their activities. They pursued the theory of "no peace beyond the line," that is, outside Europe.

Piracy, practiced openly, and repeatedly, by the Providence Islanders after the peace was signed, provoked Spain's reprisal. In June 1635, a Spanish fleet attacked the British settlement on Tortuga Island, killing every person there and burning their buildings. Tortuga, or Tortue, is a small island lying close to and off the northwest shore of Hispaniola, now Haiti and the Dominican Republic.

The settlers on Providence Island heard of the massacre at Tortuga and immediately asked permission to strike back. In Britain, Providence Island Company officials approached the government and, in response to their request, King Charles I granted them new broad letters of marque. Now, widespread privateering attacks, government approved, could again be undertaken.

Upon hearing this news, Lewis Morris and Captain Axe hurried back from the Moskito Cays to Providence Island. They had been out on the cays and on the mainland nearby at Cape Gracias a Dios, Nicaragua, for nearly three years. Forthwith, Morris was reemployed by the Providence Island Company.

During the next two years, as a result of these new letters of marque, many privateers were sent out by the Providence Island Company. Some of the ships to participate were the *Blessing*, the *Expectation*, the *Hopewell*, the *Hunter*, the *Happy Return*, the *Providence*, the *James*, the *Mary Hope*, the *Spy* and the *Swallow*. Captain Sam Axe commanded the *Swallow* in 1638. Morris was aboard the *Swallow* as navigator.

By 1639, Lewis Morris and Captain Axe were back in London planning a new voyage. Again, their employer was the Providence Island Company, which was doing well with its new and exclusive franchise for privateering in the Caribbean.

For this voyage, the company chartered the ship *Mary* from the successful merchant, Maurice Thompson, of London.[2] A letter, written in June 1639, to Captain Nathaniel Butler, the new governor of Providence sent there in 1638, gave the reason for sending out the *Mary*. The owners of the Providence Island Company in London had received information that great quantities of silver ore had been discovered in the Bay of Darien area between East Panama and northwest Columbia, then called "New England" by the British.

In commissioning the *Mary*, Sam Border was designated master of the vessel until it reached Providence Island. At Providence, Captain John Brent was to take command of the *Mary*. What rank Lewis Morris was to hold is not known except that the letter to Governor Butler stated that "Captains Axe and Brent, Lewis Morris and Sam Border are joined with the Governor in this employment."[3]

Instructions to the group were that they should proceed to the Bay of Darien to examine the silver ore deposit. If the ore was genuine and of good quality, the *Mary* should return to England with a full cargo. If not of good quality, the owners added with sound (but not very Puritan) business sense, "The ship may be employed for prize for one month." Then, probably in reference to Morris' and Axe's privateering background, the owners wrote a special letter stating the hope that the employees will "take a course which becomes a faithful servant," and requesting further a forebearance of "all private design."[4]

The *Mary* left England in July 1639. At Barbados, their first scheduled stop, they planned to take on reinforcements, then proceed to Providence Island to let off two Puritan families and some servants, about thirty in all. But the *Mary* had hardly cleared the English channel on the first leg of her voyage down to Cape Cantin, Africa when she was attacked and captured by north African Barbary Corsairs.

The *Mary* with her crew and passengers was sailed to the port of Algiers by her captors, where all aboard were imprisoned and put to hard labor as slaves. The port of Algiers, in 1639, when the *Mary* was taken there, was a Turkish Moslem city.

A letter written from Algiers to the Providence Island Company, by John Symonds, one of the *Mary*'s Puritan passengers, asked that the Company make every effort to ransom the passengers and crew, suggesting that "the summe will be great."[5] In the letter, Symonds related the wretched condition under which they remained in captivity. It read: "to write our misery will be tedious. . .there are some forced to filthiness, some to despair, and so to turn their backs on Christ. . . ."

This great assault on shipping by the Turks was not for ransom alone. There was a fanatical religious conflict being waged by all Moslems, or Mohammedans, against all Christians. Thus, when Puritan John Symonds wrote that some had turned their backs on Christ, he was referring to the effort by their Moslem captors to convince the English Christians to give up their religion, offering in return better living conditions and freedom from slavery. Symonds added that as far as he was concerned, he had "been much sollicited, but God hath established my hart in Christ."

Apparently Symonds was willing to listen to their solicitations, but the more reluctant ones were put to slave labor strengthening fortifications, building new prisons for additional captives, or as galley slaves, chained to their oars. As Symonds put it, "the Chaynes and hunger that some undergoe is lamentable." According to Symonds, there were 2,000 Englishmen being held at Algiers at the time that he was there.

The crew and passengers of the *Mary* remained in captivity at Algiers for over six months. Finally, in February 1640, they were ransomed by the Providence Island Company, and all returned to England.

1. CO Col. Entry Bk. Vol. III p.103–107; CSPC 1574–1660:166.
2. CO Col. Entry Bk. Vol. IV p.138–142; CSPC 1574–1660:295; CO Prov. Is. Co. Minute Bk. 124/1/149, 150.
3. CO Col. Entry Bk. Vol. IV p.138–142; CSPC 1574–1660:295; CO Prov. Is. Co. Minute Bk. 124/1/148 or 149 et seq.
4. CO Col. Entry Bk. Vol. IV p.138–142; CSPC 1574–1660:297, 298; CO Prov. Is. Co. Minute Bk. 124/1/148 or 149 et seq.
5. CO Prov. Is. Co. Minute Bk. 124/1/148 or 149; PRO 30/15/2, Manchester Papers 423; Newton 265.

3

English
Privateer

About the time Lewis Morris was being ransomed from the Turks at Algiers, a Captain William Jackson was returning to England from a very profitable privateering voyage, which had lasted two years. Captain Jackson's trip had been under the sponsorship of the Earl of Warwick's Providence Island Company, in conjunction with Maurice Thompson, merchant of London.

Jackson returned with a huge prize richly laden with indigo, which brought £3,000 to the Providence Island Company. Jackson had sold his share of the loot in North America just before returning home. Governor John Winthrop of the Massachusetts Bay Company recorded the arrival of Jackson there: "Here came a small bark from the West Indies, one Captain Jackson in her, with the commission from Westminster [Providence Island] Company to take prize, &c...from the Spaniard. He brought much wealth in money, plate, indico, and sugar. He sold his indico and sugar here for £1400 wherewith he furnished himself with commodities and departed again for the West Indies."[1]

Soon, Captain Sam Axe and Lewis Morris would be joining Captain William Jackson in a privateering expedition on a grand scale. The whole enterprise was again to be under the sponsorship of Maurice Thompson, merchant of London, in association with the Earl of Warwick and others of the Providence Island Company. Captain William Jackson was selected to be admiral of the fleet. Captain Sam Axe was named vice admiral, and Captain John Newcombe, rear admiral. An eyewitness manuscript account of this trip is still in existence, from which all events in this episode will be quoted, unless otherwise noted.[2]

Three ships were fitted out and furnished for the voyage with "all manner of warlike provision." The ships were the *Charles*, to be commanded by Admiral Jackson, the *Valentine*, by Vice Admiral Axe, and the *Dolphine* under Rear Admiral Newcombe, with "Lewis Morris Master" of the *Dolphine*. During this era, English men-of-war were usually commanded by land officers. The navigating and the sailing of vessels were in the hands of sailing masters, such as Lewis Morris.

The *Charles* was a ship of 350 tons burden and carried 28 or 30 guns. The *Valentine* was 240 tons and had 20 guns. The *Dolphine* was 140 tons with 16 guns. The three ships left England during the latter part of July or in early August 1642, and arrived at Barbados in about seven weeks. Lewis Morris did not join the fleet until it came to Barbados, having returned there from Britain shortly after his release by the Algerian corsairs.

On the fleet's arrival in Barbados, Lewis Morris took over his duties on the *Dolphine*.[3] The *Valentine*, promptly, was dispatched to St. Christopher Island to pick up Captain-Vice Admiral Axe who also had returned to the Indies from Britain after his imprisonment by the Algerians. During the ship's stay at St. Christopher, Axe was instructed to recruit men for land and sea service.

While Sam Axe was busy recruiting at St. Christopher, Lewis Morris, who was well acquainted on Barbados, was busy at the same task. As recruiting progressed, other members of the expedition were engaged in putting additional vessels into service. Three light sailing craft were rigged and fitted. Each was ten to twelve tons. They were the *Mercury*, the *Pegasus*, and the *Argus*. These light ships were necessary for giving chase to the enemy and for landing men, the bigger ships being unsuited for these close-in maneuvers.

A merchant ship from London, the *Guifte*, was hired for only four months. She was to be used as a transport to bring treasure back to London, thereby repaying Maurice Thompson.

Recruiting at Barbados was going speedily. Lewis Morris was able to convince all the personnel that was needed, with the usual stipulation, "no booty, no pay." The type of recruits obtained at Barbados during this period was described as: "bold only to do mischief, not to be commanded as soldiers, nor to be kept in any civil order; being the most profane debauched persons that we ever saw."[4] There were no uniforms for the recruits. Everyone dressed as he wished, except for the officers, who wore army uniforms, since at that time, naval dress was unknown.

Lewis Morris had been sailing the Caribbean for several years. His contribution to the venture would be a major one. He had kept a "journal"[5] of his ports of call in the West Indies, and these would be invaluable to the fleet, particularly regarding special knacks of entering harbors.

The fleet of privateers departed Barbados November 11, 1642, about a month and a half after arrival there. It was about 4:00 o'clock in the afternoon when they hoisted sail, and set a southwest course for "ye Testigoes."[6] It took three days to make the passage, and upon arrival, they found that Vice Admiral Sam Axe was already at anchor there, this being the appointed rendezvous for the two contingents of the fleet.

Axe had brought with him 250 men recruited from St. Christopher, making a total in his group of 643 men, plus officers. The whole fleet, including the Morris recruits, now consisted of seven vessels, carrying something over 1,100 men.

While the recruits were busy training at Los Testigoes with "muskitts, Carbines, Fire-locks, Half-Pikes, Swords, Cutlases, and ye like offentius weapons," one of the light ships, the *Pegasus*, was sent out on a reconnoitering mission to Margarita, a sizeable island lying close to the mainland off Venezuela, west of Trinidad. The *Pegasus* reported that it found very little shipping and no Spanish ships-of-war in the area. By the time the *Pegasus* returned, the men had been training ten days and the "Councell of Warr" decided that the Island of Margarita would be a good first test for the new recruits.

The booty obtained at Margarita was fair, including a Spanish vessel to add to the fleet. They renamed her the *Margarita*, after the island, and fitted her out with arms, captain, and crew, as well as a company of foot soldiers.

At Margarita, Captain-Admiral Jackson took aboard some native Indians, called "tawnies" by the English, to provide intelligence on harbor conditions, fortifications, and possible sources of loot. This was a favorite pirate device. Both tawnies and Negro slaves were very cooperative with the British, for the Spaniards had treated them badly, sometimes cruelly.[7]

The next destination of the fleet was to be "ye Salt Tartuga," now

Scale in Miles

Santiago de La Vega (Spanish Town)

Fort

shoals

shoals

Second Landing

First Landing

Old Harbor

Port Royal (now sunken)

JAMAICA HARBOR

Tortue

HISPANIOLA

PUERTO RICO

St. Christopher

Cape Tiburon

Jacmel

St. Lucia

Barbados

Curaçao

Cuyo Grande Is.

La Tortuga

Los Testigos

TRINIDAD

Margarita Is.

Maracaibo

Puerto Cabello

Caracas

Cumana

PLATE 1

GKM

La Tortuga, lying just to the west of Margarita. The fleet planned to take on water here while waiting for the return of two light vessels dispatched to scout the shore of the mainland, near the castle and garrison at Cumana, where pearl boats were supposed to lie. The report from the scouting party revealed no pearl boats in sight, so the Council of War decided to head for Caracus, now called La Guaira, being the port of modern Caracas.

One of the captives taken at Margarita had reported that there was a British ship loading at Caracas, bound for Spain. The Council of War decided that a British boat carrying Spanish goods was just as legitimate a prey as a Spanish vessel carrying Spanish goods, so they decided to take her. Approaching the port, the fleet came under the fire of three strong forts. Several shots from heavy guns were fired on both sides. The *Valentine* was hit in the mainmast and the *Margarita* in the foresail and fore-tackle. Lewis Morris was able to maneuver the *Dolphine* so that it escaped damage. Not wishing to risk so much for so little, the fleet of invaders stood off again to sea.

The next problem was to repair the *Valentine* and the *Margarita*. To this end, the flotilla sailed to an island the Spaniards called Catto, just west of Caracas. After the repairs were completed at Catto, the Council of War discussed where to strike next.

It was agreed that the next stop would be Puerto Cabello, not far distant and on the mainland. Here they landed at dusk with two hundred men. Near the dock there was a broad savanna where the men spread out in a long line and marched across the open ground toward the town with all armament displayed, shouting and waving cutlasses in storybook fashion. Sailors, under sailing officers, led the beach landing, and Lewis Morris was in the vanguard.

Approaching a narrow street, the sailors closed ranks and proceeded up the hill where the fort was situated. There was considerable small arms fire from both sides and two of the landing party were killed. By this time it was becoming dark, so the sailors returned to the landing site.

Under the cover of night, after the sailors had done their job, many foot soldiers were landed. Then at daybreak, the entire force marched directly to the fort without opposition. Discovering that the fort was deserted, the force marched five miles inland. Here they found beautiful plantations, but no people. Everything had been removed from the houses, leaving bare floors. In retaliation for this "discourtesy," as they called it, the invaders destroyed the religious objects in the cathedral and carried away its bells.

The next port of call was the Island of Curacao, called "Carrisall." It was a Dutch settled island, off the northwest coast of Venezuela, where the inhabitants were not friendly with the Spaniards. Thus, the fleet was allowed good anchorage while taking on water and provisions, for which they gave plate in barter.

When well stocked with provisions, the fleet set sail for Maracaibo, called "Mericao." The ships rounded Paraguana Peninsula and sailed down the Gulf of Venezuela, then anchored three or four leagues off the great bar that separates the Gulf of Venezuela from Lake Maracaibo. The next day they departed this anchorage, leaving behind Captain-Admiral Jackson. His ship, the *Charles*, was the largest vessel in the fleet, and it drew too much water to take the risk of the shallow passage into Lake Maracaibo. Even the smaller vessels were to find it difficult to avoid the sandbars. It took three days to get to Maracaibo. Lewis Morris, sailing the *Dolphine*, made the winding passage without difficulty.

At Maracaibo the Spaniards had eight days notice that the invaders were in the area and they welcomed Jackson and his fleet with determined shore fire. Nonetheless, at daybreak, a landing was made and the town was secured with the loss of only two lives. Some loot was taken, but much of the town's valuables had been carried to the hills. The most important plunder seems to have been "100 butts of Sack [large casks of dry wine] to make merry at our night approaching Christmas."

There was drinking and wenching by the crew where either could be found. Many of the residents of Maracaibo were killed, and those who survived spent the days before Christmas praying for the dead, as well as for the marauders to leave. But the invaders did not leave. They stayed in Maracaibo sending out foraging and scouting parties. Some went inland, with considerable profit.

Four days after Christmas, the Spaniards petitioned for a truce so as to bury their dead. The invaders decided this was a ruse to give the Spaniards time to transport their treasures farther inland, and the request was initially denied. Then a temporary truce was granted. At the same time, however, parties were sent out to search for goods, which they found in abundance.

After being in control of Maracaibo for a complete month, the invaders agreed to give up the town on payment of a ransom of 10,000 pieces of eight. In addition, they took a few prisoners, and forced the inhabitants to reprovision the fleet. Four vessels constituted part of the prize. They renamed these the *Mericao* (again in honor of the town), the *Swallow*, the *Swifte*, and the *Spy*. The marauding fleet now numbered an even dozen.

Following one more attack at the lower end of Lake Maracaibo, the fleet sailed back up the lake toward the Gulf of Venezuela, arriving alongside Captain-Admiral Jackson's vessel, the *Charles*, just about two months after leaving her.

The fleet then set sail, February 22, 1643, bound for "ye Salt Ponds," just north of Caracas, now called Cayo de Sal and Cayo Grande. Enroute, extreme weather was encountered and the fleet was separated. The *Swifte* was forced upon the lee shore of Venezuela, dashed among the rocks and wrecked. The men escaped with their lives, but were captured and turned over to the Spanish governor of Caracas.

The *Margarita* proved so leaky during the storm that every moment it was expected that she would go under. When it appeared almost certain that the *Margarita* was about to be lost with all hands on board, Lewis Morris sailed the *Dolphine* alongside. Somehow, in the raging storm, Lewis Morris boarded the *Margarita* to examine her damage. He found a hole in her hull considerably below the water line. All efforts to plug the hole from the inside proved futile.

Finally Lewis Morris, with a line around his waist, went overboard and successfully stuffed the hole from the outside. An eye witness to this act said that the ship and its crew were saved "by God's mercy assisting ye industry of one Lewis Morris, Master of the Dolphine who by diveing under water stopped ye Leake...."

1. Winthrop 1:307.
2. Camden 3:34.
3. Caribbeana 5:84.
4. Venables XXVI.
5. Morris RHM 1763 Corres.
6. These islands are now called Los Testigoes, lying off the coast of Venezuela on the lower end of the Lesser Antilles. They consisted of nothing but several tiny barren and rocky islands, without inhabitants.
7. A contemporary account of conditions on Margarita explained, "The Spaniards with inhumane cruelty taught the negroes to dive for pearls; for those who were not nimble or dexterous enough, they beat unmercifully, dropt scalding wax or scalding oyl upon them or stigmatised them with hot irons." (America 627)

4

Jamaica
Captor

Following the violent storm, six ships of the fleet of eleven reached "ye Salt Ponds," their planned destination, including Lewis Morris in the *Dolphine*, and the *Margarita*, which Lewis Morris had saved. The six vessels remained there for four days waiting for the others, but none arrived. It was then agreed that the missing vessels must have been blown to the north. Everyone was downcast, but all were resolved to proceed north to scout the southern coast of Hispaniola for any trace of survivors.

After a passage across the Caribbean, the reduced fleet sighted land at "Porto Jacoma," probably Jacmel, Haiti, whereupon they ran west along the coast searching every creek and harbor. Luckily, they came first upon the *Mericao*, then the *Guifte*. The crews of both vessels had gone through misery and starvation before they had reached the coast of Hispaniola. To sustain life, they had resorted to eating boiled hides, which had been seized as loot. The other missing ships were never found.

In a remarkably short time the memory of the storm and its hardships was supplanted by the desire of all to accomplish what they had set out to do. A Council of War was held as the fleet lay anchored just off "Cape Tiberon," the southwesternmost point of the Island of Hispaniola. This is now Cape Carcasse, near the town of Tiberon (the shark).

During the Council of War, it was decided to throw all caution aside and to invade the large and comparatively well populated island of Jamaica, then held by Spain. The fleet left Tiberon and proceeded to Navassa, a small island halfway between Hispaniola and Jamaica. At

17

Navassa, they captured a small vessel of twenty-five tons and renamed her the *Joseph*.

On March 25, 1643, the fleet appeared off Jamaica at the entrance of the island's principal harbor, now Kingston Harbor.[1] One gun was fired to bring the ships together, and shortly thereafter a landing party was put ashore on the west side of the harbor. The party started moving along the shore but found no road, whereupon they captured two natives and took them back aboard ship. On questioning them, it was found that there was a road leading to the city a little farther up the bay.

The next morning a landing party was made at a different spot inside the main harbor. On reaching the beach, the party was fired at from the bushes by snipers, who were soon forced to retire to a small fort.

The landing party was then charged upon from the fort by cavalry, who tried to overrun them. Small shot was played effectively and so rapidly by the invaders, that the cavalry soon lost heart and retreated. In the fight, five of the landing party were killed and eight were wounded, all of whom died shortly thereafter.

This loss of life angered the invaders and they decided to storm the fort to which the cavalry had retired. While they were organizing a frontal attack, the defenders, having no taste for such fierce battle, fled.

After entering the fort, five companies set out to take the town, leaving one company behind to hold the fort, which was not far from the landing site. Along the path leading to the town, they were constantly fired upon from the bushes.

Soon they came to a river, where they saw in a clearing another fort with two guns trained on them. They were fired upon by these guns, which were filled with rusty nails and other scrap. Here one was killed.

The five companies then divided, two of them going to the rear of the fort. Apparently the defenders did not like this maneuver for they fled while this circling movement was in process. The five companies then entered the fort and pried the big guns off their emplacements and dumped them down a bank into the river below.

The next task of the invaders was to take the town, which was accomplished without additional resistance. The townspeople had heard of the fleet's presence in the area some eight days earlier and had time to hide much of their valuables. However, some prize worth taking was uncovered.

The town itself was found to be charming. It was called Santiago de La Vega, now Spanish Town. There were four hundred to five hundred houses in the place, built for the most part out of cane plastered with mortar or lime, then covered with tile. There were five or six stately churches and one Franciscan monastery. The town was situated on the descent of a spacious plain, on the northwest of which ran a pleasant river that emptied into the harbor about four miles eastward from where the fleet lay at anchor.

Some of the men wanted to quit the whole venture and settle here, but this idea was quickly squelched by the Council of War. However, twenty-three sailors and twelve soldiers soon thereafter deserted. Later, the deserters were caught, tried, and two were executed. The others were pardoned.

Such wholesale desertion soon convinced the Council of War that the armada should get back into action as soon as possible. Terms of ransom for the town were agreed upon, including provisions and 17,000 pieces of eight. By this time, Lewis Morris was taking a leading part in the Council of War.

After supplies were taken aboard, the fleet set sail eastward toward Hispaniola, but they encountered foul weather during which the *Guifte* and the *Margarita* were separated from the others. The balance of the fleet returned to Jamaica.

This time the flotilla put in at another harbor, probably Old Harbor Bay, where they boarded and captured a Spanish vessel. After putting the Spanish ashore and manning the ship with their own men, the fleet headed west, touching the westernmost tip of Jamaica at Point Negrillo (meaning Black Poplar), now South Negril Point.

From Point Negrillo they set sail for "Chimanos," now Grand Cayman, an island south of Cuba and northwest of Jamaica. Here, to everyone's joy, the recently separated *Guifte* and *Margarita* were found riding at anchor.

A Council of War was again called and the next place of attack was discussed. Some had tired of the long ordeal and wanted to divide up the spoils and go home; others wanted to continue.

After long argument, two hundred were assigned to the *Guifte* and allowed to return to Barbados, or any other British port where they might find safety. The departing group was headed by Major William Rous, not one of the discontented, but an officer who was returning home for personal reasons.

During the discussion as to where to attack next, Lewis Morris was in favor of the Honduras-Nicaragua area because he had spent three years there and he knew the waters well. He also knew native tawnies who would be willing to provide needed intelligence as to the location of loot. When the decision was made in favor of Honduras and Nicaragua, fifty or sixty sailors, together with some soldiers, deserted in the ship *Mericao*.

The first step in the new plan was to reorganize and consolidate the striking power, using only the best vessels. The *Swallow*, by reason of her leaky condition, was destroyed and all provisions and armament transferred to the prize taken at Jamaica, which they had since renamed the *Swann*.

At about this time, Lewis Morris was promoted from sailing master to the rank of captain and was given command of one of the vessels of the fleet—which one is not known.

After getting shipshape again, the armada left Grand Cayman and steered a course directly for Cape Gracias a Dios, the former home port of Lewis Morris, in his Moskito Cays tenure. The fleet, however, was blown off its planned course and made landfall considerably north and west of the Cape. Because of this, it was decided to run up to Roatan Island, then occupied by the British, and located off the coast of Honduras.[2]

On arrival in friendly waters at Roatan, the Council of War sent out the usual scouting party to capture some prisoners and from them to gather any information that might prove valuable regarding sources of loot. The scouting party captured and questioned some natives but they later escaped. They did, however, bring back information that two ships from Spain were due at "Truxilo," now Trujillo, on the mainland nearby. These ships were supposed to be carrying arms and ammunition, together with other valuable cargo. The fleet had hoped to proceed from Roatan to San Pedro Salu, but it was now decided to act on the intelligence just received.

A landing was promptly made two or three miles below the town of Trujillo. Resistance was negligible and plundering went on while they awaited the arrival of the two Spanish ships about which they had learned from the natives. Within a short time the two ships were sighted, and a chase began. Unfortunately for the attackers, a fog descended and the prey got away. For ten days, search was conducted by five light vessels of the fleet, but the two Spanish vessels were never sighted again. A small ship was taken, however, which was fitted up as a man-of-war, and renamed the *Content*.

As the chase was in progress, the remainder of the fleet stayed at anchor in the harbor. While there, a "horrible sickness" came over the men and twelve died. When the pursuit party returned, it was decided to depart because, what they described as the plague, was increasing. Before sailing, they broke up the *Joseph* and rigged another small ship, which they renamed the *Exchange*.

The destination was to be Cape Gracias a Dios, where Lewis Morris would be able to provide treatment and comfort for the dying. They could not go to Providence, for it was back in the hands of the Spaniards. Upon the fleet's arrival at the Cape, the Indians soon learned that Lewis Morris was aboard. They came out in their canoes to visit him, as he had been their good friend when he had lived among them. The best care available was provided for the sick, but they grew no better, whereupon the fleet departed for the Moskito Cays, another former residence of Morris.

Here, the sick were taken ashore where Lewis Morris supervised the building of small individual huts for each man to lie in. Morris then sent the Indians out to catch turtle, which was prepared and given to the men. Morris felt sure that a diet of fresh turtle would help cure the ailing. On a diet of turtle the men soon improved.

When the sick had completely recovered, which illness may have been beriberi and was cured by eating vitamin-rich turtle, it was decided to set sail for the Gold Coast, in search of more loot. Enroute, the fleet stopped for a few days at The Corn Islands off southern Nicaragua, a frequent port of call by Morris in earlier days. Here they sent out their usual scouting party. Satisfied with reports brought back, and while running south, they struck at several places along the coast. At one landing a foraging party was seized and eaten by cannibals.

After this disaster, there was little stomach for this uncivilized area. The fleet then sailed east along the coast of Panama, past Portobelo to the "Bay of Talon," now the Bay of Tolu in Columbia. A landing was made here, and with only the exchange of a slight volley, the port was won.

The town provided an unexpected store of riches. There was plate, jewels, linen, sack and sugar. After the invaders took what they wanted, the smaller ships made a trip up the Sinu River. On this short journey, four men were lost in an attack.

Having now been out over a year, some of the men were greatly fatigued, and the Council of War decided to head for a little island off the south coast of Cuba, where the weather and other conditions afforded a place to rest and to go over their ships, which by this time were showing urgent need of repair. Specifically, their destination was to be the "Caias" or Cays, lying east of Isle De Pinos.

Enroute, the fleet passed Cartagena and the ships were off Santa Maria (Santa Marta) two days before the Christmas of 1643. Because of foul weather, it was not until well into January that they arrived off Point Negrillo (Negril), the westernmost point of Jamaica.

They stayed eighteen days at Negrillo. Here they cut timber for boat repairs. Then they set out for the Cays, but they were blown off course to the north, and soon were at Cape Cruz, Cuba. The water was so shallow from the Cape to the Cays that the fleet had to drop anchor every night. It took almost all of February to sail from Negrillo to "Cayo Columbo," which is probably the island now called Cayo Largo.

Here the ships were emptied and shelters for the prize cargo were set up on shore. Tents were pitched and little log houses built. Forges, for smiths and armorers, were erected. Iron bolts and nails were fashioned and timbers were cut. Neither pitch nor tar for caulking and trimming were available, but seal oil, taken as plunder, was tempered with lime made from clam shells as a substitute.

Apparently the *Dolphine* did not need major repairs for she was dispatched in search of turtle—as meat for future voyages. Lewis Morris was no longer sailing master on the *Dolphine*—he was now captain of his own ship. While on this mission for turtle, the *Dolphine* came upon the *Mericao*, which had deserted the year before. The crew of the *Mericao* was anxious to be taken back into the fold. This wish was granted, and all returned to the Cay to join the fleet.

After four months spent repairing ships, the fleet set off again for

Grand Cayman, where the victualers salted down their turtle. This done, they set sail for Cape Catoche at the end of Yucatan Peninsula, Mexico. Arriving at the Cape, they sailed down the Gulf of Mexico—then disaster hit.

The *Valentine*, the *Mericao*, and the *Swann* suddenly struck the rocks and shoals off three small desert islands, called the "Lezarechos." These were probably the Arrecifes Triangulos Islands. All three ships sank rapidly but no lives were lost.

The remainder of the fleet, with all hands aboard, proceeded to "The River Tabasco." This river is in Mexico and is now known as the Rio Grijalva. It flows into the Bay of Campeche at Alvero Obregon. The river Tabasco was entered in small boats and its current was found swift. Three towns were plundered on the way up the stream, the farthermost being Villa Hermosa, seventy miles from the mouth.

The take was good. It included five vessels in which were found one hundred and sixteen bales thought to be valuable cochineal, with some plate, hides, tallow, and campeche wood. It was one of the bales of cochineal that was later to cause conflict between Captain-Admiral Jackson and Captain Lewis Morris.

After sacking Villa Hermosa, the fleet proceeded up the Yucatan Peninsula, stopping at Champoton and Sihocac, two Indian villages. Here were found beautiful churches and antique plate (probably silver chalices, bowls, etc.) believed by the freebooters to have predated the Cortes voyage.[3] Much of this ancient plate was taken, as were great quantities of corn. At this point, it was decided to end the long campaign because the treasure had been good at last. On Wednesday, September 12, 1644, which was not far from the second anniversary of the beginning of the voyage, the fleet set sail for the straits of Florida.

On the trip across the Gulf of Mexico, the fleet was becalmed for many days, and all aboard suffered great misery from lack of water. Then, a storm arose and the ships were separated. Four vessels, including those of Jackson and Morris touched Cuba at Matanzas, then headed for Bermuda, where they arrived October 27th. They stayed in Bermuda twelve weeks disposing of their merchandise; then they weighed anchor for England, arriving in the Downs, March 6, 1645.

During the storm in the Gulf of Mexico, one segment of the fleet (probably intentionally) fell off to the southwest by way of Cuba and Hispaniola, arriving at St. Christopher on February 14, 1645. Here, the West Indies volunteers debarked. Possibly the Barbadians who were on Morris' ship had transferred to the Barbados bound vessels at the time of the calm.

During the twelve-week stay in Bermuda, the Jackson-Morris segment of the fleet divided up its share of the treasure. In this process, Jackson and Morris quarreled.

Jackson had a long record of sharp dealing on such occasions. On his return from his 1638–40 voyage of plunder, he was involved in a continuous series of law suits with members of his crew, as well as with his backers. In the present case, it appears that Jackson temporarily won the decision over Morris by denying Morris his commission to captain his own vessel from Bermuda to England, unless he agreed to sign a bond, payable to Jackson in the amount of £400.

Morris signed, but he was not one to give in easily. When he arrived in England and the bond came due, he refused to honor it. Jackson then produced the unpaid bond in magistrate's court and Morris was thrown in prison for debt.

From his prison cell, Captain Morris appealed to the House of Lords as follows: ''Your petitioner who has been employed for 15 years in the West Indies, was denied his commission to return hither by Captain Jackson, Commander-in-Chief there, until he enter into bond £400 for a bale of cochineal taken of Jackson by Captain Cromwell at 40 shillings per pound, and to become payable within two months after Cromwell or your petitioners arrival, the cochineal proved to be silvester, and not worth four shillings a pound, and yet one Poiston has in Jackson's name arrested petitioner, and now remains in the Poultry Compter. Prays for his discharge.''[4]

Shortly thereafter, Captain Morris was discharged from prison and the matter of his bond to Jackson was ''left to the law.'' This undoubtedly meant that some doubt was cast on the validity of Jackson's charges and that Jackson would be compelled to bring civil suit against Morris in order to collect on the bond.

1. Kingston was not in existence then; it was settled almost fifty years later.
2. Roatan had been occupied five years earlier, in 1638, by Captain William Claiborne, who had come to America in 1621 or 1622 as royal surveyor for the Virginia colony. Within a few years, he returned to England to organize a company of his own in which Maurice Thompson, merchant of London, was one of the principals. On his return to America in 1631, Claiborne settled Kent Island, across the Chesapeake from Annapolis, Md., which city was not settled until 1648. By 1638, Claiborne was being charged with piracy and murder. This was the same year he settled Roatan. Newton 182, 315; Lindsay 46 et seq.; Plantagenet; Md. Hist. Mag. 1931:26:381 et seq.
3. In 1519, one hundred and twenty-five years earlier, Hernando Cortes, in his conquest of Mexico for Spain, had landed at Tobasco where he found great riches and a vast empire well organized and ruled by a Sovereign, Montezuma.
4. Camden 3:34. Captain Cromwell may have been the John Cromwell mentioned in *Thirty Dunstable Families*. Stearns 16; Winthrop 2:263, 264. Poiston may have been Captain Royston, who delivered up his commission about the time of the desertion of the fifty or sixty men in the ship *Mericao*. Cochineal is a dyestuff consisting of dried bodies of female scale insects native to Mexico and South America. It is used as a reddish purple coloring, especially for cloth, and it was highly prized. In Spanish, silvestre means rustic or uncultivated, suggesting that the cochineal was not properly processed or prepared. Poultry Compter was the name of a London prison.

5

Barbadian Planter

Five years before the Jackson voyage began, while operating as a privateer out of Barbados, Lewis Morris came to the decision that he must give up the dangerous life as a privateer as soon as possible. He did not fear for his own life, but he now had a new compelling responsibility.

In 1637, Lewis Morris had married at Barbados, Anne Barton, the young widow of Thomas Barton of Barbados.[1] After his marriage, acquiring wealth so that he could provide for his bride became very important to this young man, still in his twenties. As he put it, he wished to gain enough wealth so that if anything happened to him, he could "leave an estate clear for his wife."[2]

To the end of increasing his wealth, Lewis Morris decided to remain at sea, at least for a few more years. In 1639, his first big post marriage venture almost brought him disaster, and no wealth, after being captured and imprisoned by African Corsairs. The Jackson voyages from 1642 to 1644, however, put him well on the way to financial independence.

Thus, Lewis Morris was able to make his break with the sea in 1646 or 1647 by the fortunate occurrence of a business opportunity. This opportunity was in sugar. Although sugar cane had long been a product of Barbados, it had been used mainly as a source of a liquid sweetener for a refreshing tropical drink. Some refined sugar was used by wealthy English Barbadians in their tea, but the product was not comparable to that which we know today. It was a very inferior gummy substance with a brown molasses cast to it.

Knowledge of an improved sugar refining process is said to have been brought to Barbados about 1646 by James Drax, who showed a

27

few of his friends how to refine sugar in a new and spectacular way. Lewis Morris, a neighbor of James Drax, was one of the few men who was told this secret, and soon it was to make Lewis Morris rich.

James Drax showed these few friends, how, by letting the canes of sugar ripen in the field for 15 months, instead of 12, then by boiling the extracted liquid until it had a creamy white consistency—and, finally, in a process called "claying the sugar," a product could be produced that was virtually free of molasses.

Claying the sugar was accomplished by placing the gummy molasses substance into teat shaped porous earthen molds about 12 inches long and about 4 inches across the top, covering the top of each mold with a layer of clay. Water was then slowly percolated through the clay, and in time, the water displaced much of the molasses in the sugar. When these so called "loaves" of sugar were taken from their earthen containers, the top part of the loaf was granular, white, and virtually free of molasses and called "clayed sugar." The lower part of the loaf, which still had some brown cast to it, was called "muscavado sugar."

For several years, the few Barbadian friends of Colonel Drax were able to keep the secret of their claying process before it spread to other people and other parts. Barbadian sugar became in great demand all over the world, and Lewis Morris exploited this advantage to its fullest.

Lewis Morris soon became one of the prime movers in this great clayed sugar boom, not only as a planter, but even more important as a merchant and shipper of sugar products. During one year alone, Lewis Morris shipped out of Barbados nearly a half million pounds of sugar in his fleet of ten vessels, which were named the *Samuel*, the *Supply*, the *Patience*, the *Honour*, the *Concord*, the *Charles*, the *Elizabeth*, the *White Fox*, the *Submission* and the *Beginning*.[3]

Lewis Morris was not only becoming rich, but he was becoming respectable. He was referred to as one of the "eminent planters of Barbados."[4] His home plantation was called a "lovely estate."[5] In addition to his home plantation, he had extensive sugar acreage in St. Joseph's, which was a windward parish of the island.[6]

His operation soon became so vast and so diversified that Morris persuaded his younger brother, Richard, to enter business with him in Barbados.[7]

Lewis Morris also began to take an active part in Barbadian govern-

PLATE 2

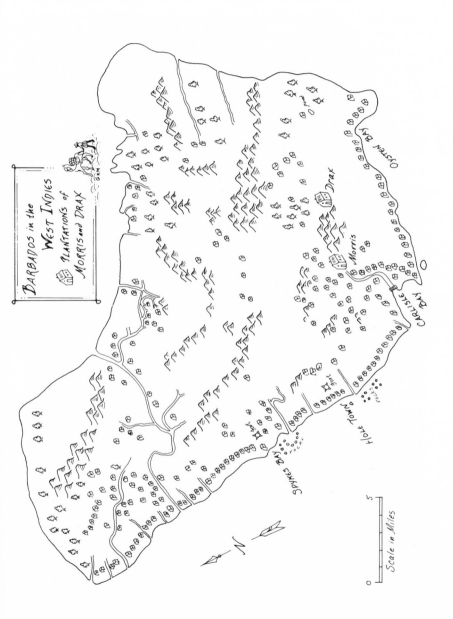

mental affairs, and within a ten year period after he had left the sea, Lewis Morris was elected to the Barbados "Assembly." Soon thereafter he was chosen by the Governor to sit on the governing "Concell of Select Men" of the island. As indicated in the Barbados Council Minute Book the: "Governor and Council took into consideration the election of a person to fill up the Council and do Order that Lewis Morris be sent to sit as a member thereof at the next meeting."[8]

The same drive and energy that Lewis Morris had displayed in fighting was now being transferred to building a place for himself in the agricultural, business and civic life of Barbados.

---

1. Caribbeana 5:84
2. Thurloe 3:249 et seq.
3. Morris 1677 Account.
4. CO Col. Papers Vol. XXX #42, 42I, 42II, 42III; CSPC 1669-1674:497.
5. Thurloe 3:25; CSPC 1669-1674:497.
6. Caribbeana 5:84; Journal, Allyne Pedigree.
7. Barbados Wills 8:132; Andrews 2:8, 9 note 2.
8. Lucas 1:125; Journal Aug. 1943:177.

6

Roundhead Leader

Lewis Morris' steady rise in Barbadian political circles would soon be interrupted by civil war, which came first to England, with Charles I being supplanted by Oliver Cromwell who replaced the royalist government with a parliamentary government.

Just as there were royalist versus parliamentary supporters in England, so were there in her colonies. In Barbados, Governor Philip Bell tried to steer a neutral course between Royalists and Parliamentarians, for which he had good reason. The Royalists of Barbados far outnumbered the parliamentary people, even though Oliver Cromwell and the Parliament firmly controlled the home government of Britain.

Lewis Morris was one of the parliamentary or "Roundhead" leaders of Barbados. Humphrey Walrond was the leader of the Royalists in Barbados, called "Cavaliers." Walrond and his followers not only tried to drive all parliamentary men out of government in Barbados but did everything possible to destroy them. At first, Walrond and his group were compelled to operate within the framework of the government, namely the Assembly and the Council of Barbados under Governor Bell.

Finally, Walrond succeeded in getting through the Assembly a resolution to banish all parliamentary sympathizers. James Drax, a member of the Assembly, along with Lewis Morris, suggested as an alternative to Walrond's resolution, that Governor Bell call for a new election of the Assembly. The Governor agreed, considering this to be a compromise between the two groups, which probably would be acceptable to both.

Governor Bell underestimated Walrond's determination. When the intended election was announced, Walrond was furious and walked out of the Assembly. Civil war thus came to Barbados in the year of 1649, about seven years after it had come to England. Governor Bell promptly organized a militia to maintain order. James Drax was made lieutenant colonel and Lewis Morris captain of militia.

Inasmuch as the Royalists predominated on the island, Walrond soon was able to sway Governor Bell into signing a peace favorable to the Royalists. Forthwith, in May 1650, twenty persons who "labored the ruine of those loyally affected to his majesty" were ordered arrested.[1] This list included Captain Lewis Morris. But, before he could be apprehended, Morris escaped to England.

What influence Morris was able to exert in England is not a matter of record, but soon a parliamentary fleet of seven ships was being readied to go to the West Indies to subdue Barbados, which was still held by the Royalists. This fleet was under the command of Sir George Ayscue. Captain Lewis Morris was to be a passenger with the fleet.[2]

In a last minute change of tactics, Ayscue's fleet, with Morris and several other returning Barbadians aboard, was ordered to support Admiral Robert Blake in his effort to bring the Scilly Islands (off Lands End, England) under control before the fleet proceeded to Barbados. As ordered, a fleet of twenty-two ships, together with long boats for landing 2,500 foot soldiers departed from Plymouth, April 12, 1651.

The fleet arrived off the Scillys on April 13th. The Royalists there were under the command of Sir John Grenville. Part of the defending force was on the Island of St. Marys, where there was a strong castle on the western side of St. Marys. Another part of the force, which included Sir John Grenville, was at New Grimsby, on the Island of Tresco, which lay a mile or two to the northwest of St. Marys.

Admiral Blake decided to make his first attack on Tresco Island at New Grimsby, which had a fine harbor, and would provide a sheltered base for the parliamentary fleet, while the balance of the islands could be taken.

When the fleet arrived off New Grimsby, they saw that the harbor was protected by two royalist men-of-war. One attempt was made to engage them, but an easterly wind prevented full contact with the enemy. Because the wind continued from the east, a Council of War was held, and Admiral Blake decided to change tactics, and to land on

PLATE 3

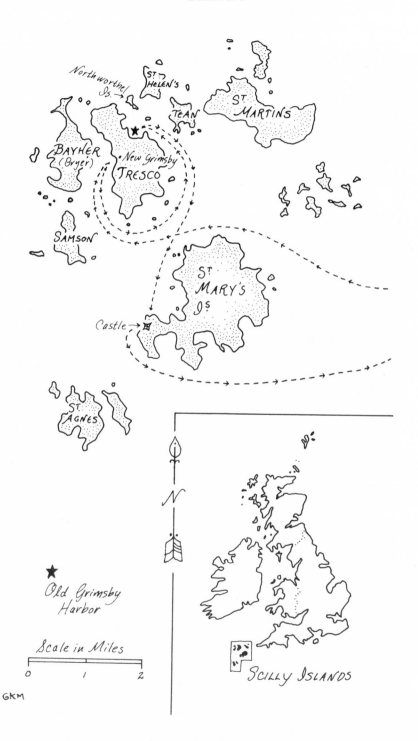

Northworthel Is. →
ST. HELEN'S
TEAN
ST. MARTINS
BAYHER (Bryer)
New Grimsby
TRESCO
SAMSON
 St. MARY'S Is
Castle →
St. AGNES
N

★
Old Grimsby Harbor

Scale in Miles
0   1   2

GKM

SCILLY ISLANDS

the opposite or the eastern side of Tresco Island, at Old Grimsby Harbor, then infrequently used.

At six in the morning on the 17th, the wind having subsided somewhat, a determined effort was made to land at Old Grimsby. Forty boats were sent toward shore, but the force consisted of green recruits who did not know how to row. They were quickly fatigued and many became seasick. The tide ran so swiftly that only one boat reached shore on Tresco. Blake and Ayscue saw the whole debacle from the deck of Blake's flagship.

Admiral Blake demanded that the next assault on Tresco Island be made under the supervision of someone with beach landing experience. Captain Lewis Morris, a seasoned veteran, received the assignment, although he was but a passenger with the fleet.[3]

Captain Morris' first action was to consolidate his forces, some having landed on Northworthel after the first assault on Tresco, and some having sought refuge on Tean Island.[4] Three companies were taken from Northworthel to Tean, leaving only eighty men on Northworthel. This was done during the evening darkness. The eighty men left on Northworthel were instructed to keep fires burning and to make sufficient noise so that the enemy on Tresco would believe that a major force still remained on Northworthel.

When Captain Morris arrived on Tean, he found that the men there had lost their morale and were unwilling to make a second assault on Tresco. During the night, however, a new spirit was instilled in the invasion force. According to one of the sailors in the force, it amounted to "an alteration even unto admiration, declaring their readiness for a second attempt."[5]

In his account, this same sailor was not sure what had brought the men around, but he seems to have given credit partly to prayer, partly to fresh victuals, and partly to the presence of Captain Morris and his two hundred sailors, who this time would row the soldiers ashore, in fact would lead them ashore. No attempt was made to hide the fact that a contingent was on Tean. Fires were kept burning there throughout the first night and the next day and evening. Then, at about eleven o'clock at night, the large force on Tean began to enter boats under the cover of a smoke screen, which seems to have been accomplished by smudging the fires.

Landing at night had been a technique perfected by Morris during his privateering days in the Caribbean. Fortunately the water was calm, with only a slight breeze blowing from the northeast. The smoke from the fires on Tean drifted slowly toward Tresco, providing cover for the landing force. In the words of one of the soldiers who took part in the landing, "the smoke where of was blown towards the enemy which somewhat obscured our passage; yet the enemy discovered us when we came about half way over, and took an alarum, and ere we attained the shore fired many ordnance upon us, which did no hurt . . . The boats came up for the most part together, and put to the shore where the enemy disrupted our landing with stout resistance, insomuch as the seamen were forced back into the water."[6]

Captain Lewis Morris "was the first to land," followed by seamen who, after being driven back into the water and coming on again, valiantly held their ground until soldiers landed to reinforce them.[7]

Sir John Grenville escaped from Tresco Island to St. Marys Island, leaving behind provisions, ammunition, and the frigates, the *Mitchell* and the *Peter*, which were guarding Tresco's New Grimsby Harbor.[8] Grenville proposed an exchange of prisoners, but Blake refused. Five days later, on June 2, 1651, Blake demanded surrender, and Grenville acceded.

As a reward for his extreme bravery and resourcefulness during the assault at Old Grimsby Harbor, Captain Lewis Morris was invited to participate in the surrender negotiations.[9]

Henry Leslie, Bishop of Downs, who was in the Scilly Islands at the time, gives this Royalist view of both landings: "and so on the 17th day they landed forth many shallops, having a brass piece charged with case shot in the forepart, but they were so valiantly resisted that they were forced to retreat, their admiral being shott through and through and driven to ship his cable, one of their shallops sunke and another so payed with small shot that she went off with towe oars; all the rest dropping into ye water.

"But on the 18th day, in the silence of the night, they [the landing force now headed by Captain Lewis Morris] having the opportunity of a great calm came on again with all their forces and after a long debate they overpowered our men with multitudes and the strength of their pikes, having the help of seamen both to lead them on and to drive on their reare, and so gained the place."[10]

After the battle, Sir George Ayscue hastened to report to the home government as follows: "so that Colonel Blake and I being Joyned, we went for Scilly, to prosecute our design on that place, which by Gods blessing, is now effected, and the Islands of Trescoe and Bryers gained for Parliament, with little loss. I must say, for the honor of our Seamen, that 200 of them designed to make good the landing for the soldiery (which indeed was the main work) did perform it resolutely being led on by Captain Morris (who is a passenger on my ship bound for the Barbados) who behaved himself very gallantly, and indeed was very much instrumental in the work, and deserves a publick acknowledgment for his good service. There were slain of the enemy about 15, and I think five of ours, and 160 or more of the enemy taken prisoners, being most of them Irish . . ."[11]

In his report, Ayscue noted further that he wished to know the pleasure of the Council so that he could proceed upon his voyage to Barbados to bring that royalist colony under control. The Council requested that Ayscue return to England before proceeding to Barbados.

Poet John Milton was publishing a pamphlet in London at the time, called Mercurius Politicus. The taking of the Scilly Islands from the Royalists caused great excitement and celebration, and Milton, as did other pamphleteers, published long articles over several issues, praising the action, and lauding Lewis Morris for his bravery.[12]

On the victorious fleet's arrival in England, it was received with great honors, as was Captain Lewis Morris. Morris was allowed to carry the terms of peace to Parliament and the Council of State granted him £100 for his "good service in Scilly."[13] Encouraged by this attention, Captain Morris was soon advising the Council on how to conduct the war against other royalist colonies, including Barbados. The Council wrote to Sir George Ayscue that they had received new intelligence on Barbados, and they suggested that Ayscue take Captain Morris' advice, which Ayscue apparently was happy to do.[14]

1. Foster 49, 50; Harlow 53.
2. Mercurius Politicus 1651:794.
3. Ibid: 788, 789.
4. Mirror 3:214, 215.
5. Special Hand 1185, 1186.
6. Lereck 10 et seq.; Special Hand 1186.
7. Mercurius Politicus 1651:793.
8. Severall Proceedings 1651:85:1291, 1292, 1293.
9. Powell 134.
10. Nicholas 1:251.
11. Mercurius Politicus 1651:788, 789.
12. Ibid.
13. PRO Dom. Council Proced. May 21, 1651; CSPD 1651:213, 258.
14. CO Interregnum Entry Bk. Vol. CXVII p.250 et seq.; CSPC 1574–1660:358, 359; PRO Dom. Council Proced. May 24, 1651; CSPD 1651:217, 274.

7

Parliamentary Soldier

After several months in England following the Scilly Islands en-
counter, Sir George Ayscue's parliamentary fleet got under way for
Barbados to subdue the Royalists there. The flotilla departed from
Plymouth August 5, 1651. Captain Lewis Morris and several other
Barbadians were again passengers with the fleet.[1] Morris was aboard
the *Rainbow*, Admiral Ayscue's flagship, so that he could be near at
hand to advise Ayscue on tactics at Barbados, as recommended by the
Council of State.

The fleet consisted of seven vessels mounting a total of 236 guns.
They were the *Rainbow*, the *Brazil*, the *Amity*, the *Success*, the *Malaga
Merchant*, the *Increase*, and the *Ruth*.[2] There were four merchant ships
with the fleet, making a total of eleven vessels.

Shortly after Sir George Ayscue was dispatched to Barbados, another fleet was readying to go to the western world.[3] Upon contacting
Ayscue at Barbados, they were to continue on to Virginia, to reduce
that royalist colony.

Ayscue was considerably delayed in his voyage across the Atlantic.
"Little winds and many calms" is the way he described the passage.
He did not arrive at Barbados until October 19th, a journey of ten
weeks and two days. However, the final day's sailing, done at night,
was splendid.

With this good sailing luck at last, Ayscue was able to surprise the
Barbadians. In Carlisle Bay, at Bridgetown, he found fifteen sails,
most of them Dutch. All Dutch vessels were seized for violating the
Navigation Act, passed by the Commonwealth the year before, which
act prohibited British colonies from trading with anyone but British
merchants.

Part of the parliamentary fleet pulled within half-musket fire of the main fort in Carlisle Bay and considerable shot was exchanged. It appears that the Morris-Ayscue strategy was first to try to bluff the Barbadians into surrender. Ayscue had told the Council of State that no rational opportunity would be lost to make "this stubborn island know their duty to the Commonwealth of England."[4]

Grandiose as were the remarks of Ayscue, he most surely had been advised by Morris that he could not successfully invade the island with his force of slightly over 2,000 men against 5,000 royalist ground troops and horse soldiers who were ready and waiting to resist any landing.

Knowing that such a large defending force awaited him, Ayscue next sent a message ashore calling upon the inhabitants "to prevent the effusion of blood and the devastation of their property by accepting timely offers of peace."[5]

Lord Francis Willoughby, then Governor of the Island in place of Bell, and a staunch Royalist, sent a message back that he would not surrender, and that he aimed to hold the island in the name of King Charles, meaning, of course, the future Charles II then in exile, and son of the executed Charles I.

Actually, Willoughby's situation was not as favorable as he thought it was. He had received false intelligence from a Dutch merchant ship, recently arrived at Barbados, that Prince Charles had landed in England and was near London, that all England had willingly and joyfully submitted to him, and that the rule of Parliament would soon end.

When Willoughby refused to knuckle under, Ayscue decided to impose a blockade around the island so that no provisions could enter, and thus he would try to starve the royalist Barbadians into surrender. Not long after the blockade had been employed, the fleet destined for Virginia arrived at Barbados, whereupon Ayscue became a little bolder. He had been off Barbados now for a month, and some aggressive action had to be taken.

No time could be lost. The Virginia fleet had suffered 200 deaths as a result of sickness on the voyage over, and the fleet was anxious to press on to North America.

A landing party was promptly organized to harass the Barbadians and to make them think that a full scale invasion by the men of both fleets was about to take place, which might make them capitulate.

Again, it was to be Captain Lewis Morris who would lead the landing. On November 22, with two hundred experienced men, Morris landed in typical Morris privateering fashion.[6] The place was on the west coast of Barbados north of Bridgetown, at The Hole or Hole Town.

Morris and his men quickly seized the small fort and took about thirty prisoners without the loss of a man. All the prisoners, as well as four cannon, were brought back to the fleet.

A few days later Morris struck again, this time at Spykes Bay. He led a force of four hundred men ashore. Ayscue had "modeled these men into a regiment, and gave the command of them to Captain Morris."[7] Most of the landing party were sailors from the fleet. The balance were Scottish prisoners captured at Worcester, plus a few Barbadians who had escaped to the fleet and were capable of contributing to the landing.

Ayscue later described the raid at Spykes Bay as follows: "On Decemb. 7 at night, I gave them order to Land which they did, and were notably received at the Landing, but it being night they thought our forces more than they were; and the seamen running in up on the Enemy hollowing and whooping in such a fierce disorder [like the Morris of privateering days] the Enemy was so amazed that after a short dispute they all ran."[8]

A more complete description of what happened at the Spykes Bay landing can be pieced together from several accounts.[9] It had been learned by Ayscue that the garrison at Spykes Bay was lightly guarded. In the early morning darkness pursuant to this intelligence, a landing was to take place. The Royalists had their intelligence as well. They had received information on the intended landing four hours before it happened, and they had rushed reinforcements to the scene.

Twelve hundred royalist troops were at the beachhead, to meet Morris and his landing party of 400. There was a wild encounter in darkness on the beach. Finally, the beach was secured by Morris and his men who, with their "hollowing and whooping," literally scared the Royalists into retreat.

Having dislodged the Royalists from the beachhead, Morris and his landing party pursued them to Fort Royal, which was stormed and taken. The fort was occupied by Morris for almost two days. Then, the sailors who had led the attack became restless and unmanageable.

They flatly refused to dig-in and try to hold the fort. Instead they insisted on returning to the fleet.

Some say that, before they left Spykes Bay, the sailors set fire to the fort and to some nearby houses, but an eyewitness who referred to himself as "a diligent observer of the times" said they did no such thing.[10] He reported that both landings, at The Hole and Spykes Bay, were made at night in typical Morris fashion and both were "wonderously successful," but not having the power to follow up the advantage, on each occasion, the forces returned to the ships "not doing any further harm which he [Morris] might have done by firing houses." Before departing Spykes Bay, on Morris' orders, four cannon were dumped into the sea so that they would be of no further use to the Royalists. All four guns were later recovered and taken to the fleet.

Captain Morris with 400 men had defeated Willoughby's 1,200 man army, and Morris was a hero once again. About 100 royalist soldiers were killed in the two days of battle. Eighty Royalists were captured and brought back to the fleet along with five hundred arms and a considerable quantity of ammunition. Only seven or eight parliamentary men were killed, but several were wounded, including Captain Lewis Morris.[11]

Successful as the raid had been in weakening the morale of the islanders, it was not a decisive battle. The Royalists still held the island. To the Royalist's further advantage, the Virginia fleet was anxious to depart. This would leave Ayscue with a much diminished force.

A plan was then devised to try to split the moderate wing from the extremist wing of the Barbadian Royalists. Humphrey Walrond, Lewis Morris' old enemy, was head of the extremists, while Colonel Thomas Modiford, Morris' friend, headed the moderates.

A letter offering very favorable terms of surrender was written aboard the *Rainbow*, and addressed to Colonel Modiford. The letter was smuggled ashore and delivered to Modiford. Soon thereafter the moderates offered a resolution in the General Assembly to accept the proposed terms of surrender. The resolution actually passed the Assembly, but Walrond amended it in such a fashion that Ayscue refused to accept it.

Modiford, on a lonely and secluded beach, then held a secret meeting with Ayscue and the several influential Barbadians with the fleet presumably including Morris.

It was one month, lacking one day, from the Spykes Bay landing, and almost three months from the fleet's arrival off Barbados, when, on January 6, 1652, Colonel Modiford gathered his regiment around him and told them of his new plan. He talked of the undesirable dictatorship of Walrond, and of the fairness of the parliamentary terms. He also spoke of Ayscue's willingness to furnish arms. Then he urged his men to join him in an alliance with the parliamentary forces.

Modiford's regiment, almost to a man, decided to cast their lot with their leader in order to bring civil war in Barbados to an end. Modiford's regiment promptly withdrew to Oysten Bay on the south shore. Here they were joined by the parliamentary forces, making up a combined army of about 2,000 foot and 100 horse soldiers. From Oysten Bay the combined forces marched seven miles inland to Modiford's home, which they converted into an armed garrison.

A few days earlier Governor Willoughby had learned of this intended defection and was preparing to strike Modiford and crush his efforts. However, so many of Willoughby's soldiers deserted him when they heard of Modiford's action, that Willoughby was forced to abandon his plan to attack.

Soon thereafter Willoughby found it necessary to surrender. Peace was signed at Mermaids Tavern, at Oysten Bay, on January 11, 1652. By the terms of this peace, all of the estates of the Parliamentarians were restored, and the estates of the Royalists left intact. All acts against The Commonwealth were pardoned, and the authority of The Commonwealth was acknowledged. After the peace, everyone went home to take up where they had left off nearly two years earlier, when civil war had come to Barbados.

As the Barbadians were returning to their homes, Ayscue wrote his report to the Council of State. He told of the bravery of Captain Lewis Morris at Barbados in much the same glowing terms he had used after Morris' heroism during the Scilly Islands encounter.[12]

As a result of his feats of bravery, Captain Lewis Morris was promoted by Oliver Cromwell to the rank of colonel.[13]

There seemed to be no rest for Morris. On June 30, 1652, about two months after Ayscue had written the Council commenting on Morris' bravery at Barbados, Morris was on his way to further service.

Parliamentary Governor Searle, who replaced Willoughby, the Royalist, wrote The Council recommending Morris for his new service in these words: "Colonel Morris whose personal valor . . . Was taken notice of, he having volunteered to command troops on a dangerous mission with the fleet."[14] The mission Colonel Morris was entering upon was to protect Barbados from possible invasion by Prince Rupert, who had sailed with his fleet to assist the royalist cause, which was still smoldering in Barbados even though the parliamentary forces were in control. To meet the threat of Prince Rupert, Governor Searle commandeered several private ships at Barbados, and put guns on them and manned them with Barbadian troops under the command of Colonel Lewis Morris.

Prince Rupert ran into difficulty as he approached the West Indies. First, he spotted a ship and chase was taken up. During the pursuit, Rupert's flagship sprung a leak. The confusion that resulted from the chase, plus the leaky vessel, caused Rupert to "over shoot" Barbados.

Rupert thereupon proceeded to the Leeward Islands of the Lesser Antilles where he spent several months doing little. Eventually Rupert and the royalist fleet returned to England without attempting to retake Barbados, whereupon Colonel Lewis Morris and his parliamentary force returned home to their families and fields.

---

1. CO Interregnum Entry Bk. Vol. CXVII p.250 et seq.; CSPC 1574–1660:358, 359; Mercurius Politicus 1651:789.
2. CO Interregnum Entry Bk. Vol. XLIV p.65; CSPC 1574–1660:349.
3. CO Interregnum Entry Bk. Vol. L p.82, 83; CSPC 1574–1660:361.
4. Mercurius Politicus 1652:1564.
5. CO Commons Jnl. Feb. 17, 1652; CSPC 1574–1660:364.
6. Mercurius Politicus 1652:1563, 1564.
7. Ibid.
8. Ibid.
9. Schomburgk 278; Davis 227, 228; Harlow 74 et seq.
10. A. B.
11. Mercurius Politicus 1652:1564.
12. Ibid: 1564, 1565.
13. Thurloe 3:250.
14. CO Interregnum Entry Bk. Vol. LVII p.50; CSPC 1574–1660:383.

8

Reluctant Cromwellian

Colonel Lewis Morris had no sooner returned to his sugar business after his pursuit of Prince Rupert, than he was again asked to serve The Commonwealth. Cromwell had seen how weak Spain was becoming in her western colonies, and he yearned to continue the Elizabethan custom of keeping pressure on Spain.

In consequence, a new and mighty campaign was planned against Spain in the West Indies. Again, the financing of the venture would be largely handled by Maurice Thompson, as some of Morris' earlier forays had been. This time the enterprise would be headed jointly by Admiral William Penn (father of William Penn of Pennsylvania) who would be the chief naval officer, and General Robert Venables, who would be in charge of ground troops. They would gather much of their arms in the West Indies and recruit about half of the personnel there.

As for tactical experience, Colonel Lewis Morris of Barbados would give the expedition this needed factor.[1] He was selected for the assignment before the fleet left England.[2] He had detailed records of the waters he earlier had sailed.[3] Everything seemed to be falling in line for the new and profitable expedition.

Sixteen or seventeen men-of-war were fitted out, together with other transports, to carry upwards of ten thousand men. Six thousand of these were recruited in England.

The fleet sailed from Portsmouth December 20, 1654. Admiral Penn did not leave until the day after Christmas so that he could spend Christmas Day with his family. The fleet arrived at Barbados on January 29, 1655, a day or two before Penn arrived, a passage of about five weeks.

Upon arrival at Barbados, to his great surprise, General Venables

43

found fourteen or fifteen Dutch sailing ships in the harbor, just as Admiral Ayscue had found four years earlier. It was a mystery to Venables why these Dutch ships were permitted to be in the harbor. After all, there had been a law enacted, the Navigation Act of 1651, which required the islanders to trade only with British merchants.

The day before Admiral Penn's arrival, General Venables had asked the Governor of Barbados to stop any Dutch ships from leaving the harbor to prevent any intelligence leaks. The Governor replied that he had no directive from Cromwell to do so. Consequently the Governor did not comply with the Venables request.

When Admiral Penn arrived, he was told that the very night before, several Dutch ships left the harbor, some laden and some empty. Penn promptly asked the Governor to come aboard and discuss the matter, but the Governor sent in his place, Colonel Thomas Modiford and Colonel Lewis Morris. "Ye Governor was said to be sick, though seen well the day before."[4]

Penn and Venables had reckoned poorly on another score. Business was thriving in Barbados since the discovery of the process of refining sugar. Consequently, recruits were not easy to come by, nor were the rewards as great as they had been in privateering days.

Further, the planters, among them Colonel Morris, were opposed to their workers going off to war and leaving the crops to rot in the fields. Consequently, they refused permission to Venables to recruit volunteers. The planters also refused to give ammunition and muskets to the expedition. They said that if they did so, they might not be able to protect themselves from the servants and slaves if many freemen were to go with the fleet.

Edward Winslow, one of the four commissioners sent over with the Penn-Venables fleet, wrote to the Secretary of the Council of State, John Thurloe, Esq., expressing his dissatisfaction with the situation. Winslow's letter to Thurloe explained it this way: "as for the 1500 muskets we are promised we should receive them here (which I ever wanted to believe) . . . but a great fear seems to be upon them lest their servants should arise when the fleet is gone because of so many of their freemen goe with us . . . We had spent many days in debate concerning the present expedition, to persuade them by all arguments we could use . . . we were forced to bluster and let them knowe that General Venables . . . was Generalissimoe of all English in America extremely broad power of which the Barbadians were not at first aware . . . and this became effectual and upon this they condescended to the beating up our drums . . . and raise our men ourselves."[5]

Colonel Morris was most reluctant to lay out the campaign for Penn and Venables as he was expected to do. Neither did he want to lead the mission. Although Morris was on the "Council of War," he told Penn and Venables that if he went along, his plantations would go to ruin.[6] Although only in his early 40s, it would be difficult for him to start over again. He spoke of high taxes and the debt he already owed the government. He felt that they should either forgive his debt, or give him some other compensation for his efforts. Here, it seems proper to quote the whole record as reported by Winslow to Thurloe:

"The reason Col. Morris will not goe with us is, because he hath to lovely an estate, which he fears may be seized for some other debts, after he is gone. At first he told us, he hoped we would forgive him a small debt he owed the state, in regard of former good services he had done them [Scilly Islands, Barbados etc.] and losses sustained for them.

"This we seemed willing, provided he went freely, knowing how necessary an instrument he might prove. This we found to be twenty six thousand nine hundred weight of sugar. Afterwards he told us in plain terms, if we would give him a hundred thousand weight of sugar, that so he may pay his debts, and leave his estate clear to his wife, then Lewis Morris would spend his blood for us.

"We told him it was beyond our commission and General Venables told him, if he [Morris] should offer up his commission he [Venables] durst not accept it, because it was sent by his highness [Cromwell] who expected so much service from him [Morris]; besides what he demanded was as much as all the field officers of the army had; and it would make them think that they were very much undervalued.

"After all this he came to me and said, there is another way, whereby we might enable him to goe with us, and presst me to move General Venables, and the rest, viz., the people of this island (saith he) never took pay for their quartering the soldiers. Now if we would bestow that on him, it would serve his turne. This I told him [I] would move, at his request, but was sure, that the General and Commissioners more prized their honor than to do it.[7]

"So this was rejected also; and the truth is he confesseth he never was where we intend first to pitch and sett downe so at last he told us, he would conceale his intention, and march his men on board the ship, for which we gave him thankes; but all these things were private as yet; but the Commissioners of the prize office have summoned him to pay his debt to the state, or shew cause.

"The truth is he prizeth himself at so high a rate, as if the expedition could not goe on without him, which made some of us in a loving way tell him, he should be glad of so experienced an instrument as he was; but with all let him know, our trust and reliance was not on him, but on God; and if the Lord would be pleased to use such an instrument in his right hand, and owne us as such, which we hoped he would, we doubted not, but we should be able to give a good account of our proceedings; and thus stands the case betwixt him and us."[8]

Lewis Morris knew that the expedition had been financed largely by Maurice Thompson. Morris knew that Maurice Thompson was a business man and Morris was certain that Thompson regarded this expedition as a commercial venture.

Further, this was not Morris' first business arrangement with Thompson. There had been many before. Now, Morris was being asked to embark on an expedition not much, if any, less commercial than any other Maurice Thompson adventure, but this time he was asked to do it, not for profit, but in the name of patriotism.

As indicated in Winslow's letter, Colonel Morris had been absolutely frank and honest when he said he knew little about Hispaniola where they were to "sett downe" first. In his voyages with Admiral Jackson, he had touched only the south shore of Hispaniola, and therefore he could not advise them from experience on a plan of battle to be conducted on the north shore.

Captain Gregory Butler, one of the Commissioners with the Penn and Venables fleet, wrote to Oliver Cromwell as follows relative to where they intended to invade: "May it please his Highness ... aboard the *Swiftsure* [Penn's flagship] a conference was held with Colonel Muddiford and Colonel Morris, the night before I set sail [from Barbados] for St. Christopher's the some of it was what place might be attempted, but indeed nothing concluded before my departure which was early the next morning ..."[9]

Despite all of the problems, in the end, Col. Lewis Morris marched his troops aboard on March 30, 1656, as he had promised.[10] There were 960 men, 120 officers, 830 rank and file, plus 10 staff officers. He then turned over his command to Colonel D'Oyley (or Dawley) who had been General Venables' lieutenant colonel, and who later became Governor of Jamaica. Lewis Morris then stepped ashore, and the fleet departed for Hispaniola.

Richard Morris, the Colonel's younger brother, helped recruit the Barbadian regiment and was to be captain of one of the companies.[11] Richard followed the example of his brother Lewis, and refused to go along on the mission.

Upon arrival of the fleet off Hispaniola a decision, regarding where to land, was still being debated. Then, almost in the middle of the operation, the landing plans were changed, and the outcome of the battle was a debacle for the British. They lost 1,700 men out of the 9,700 who landed, and they lost the battle, for which Penn and Venables were later tried.

Only five days before the fleet's departure, Colonel Lewis Morris had been elevated to the governing council of the island of Barbados, a fact which would not suggest a Governor and Council disapproval of the position Morris took in his discussions with Penn and Venables.

Although the assault on Hispaniola failed, the conquest of Jamaica, where Morris laid out the battle plan, went precisely according to the strategy laid out by Colonel Morris. They landed on the west side of the harbor, now Port Royal Harbor. Sporadic fire was encountered, which was ineffectual.[12] The landing party marched up the same road Morris had trod. They entered the town, now Spanishtown, shortly thereafter, to the great surprise of the garrison, which had expected them to land elsewhere. Not one soldier was lost in this whole affair.

 1. Lucas 1:125; Journal 4:177; Thurloe 3:249 et seq.
 2. PRO Dom. Council Proced. Dec. 16, 1654; CSPD 1654:411.
 3. Morris RHM 1763 Corres.
 4. Sea Jnl.
 5. Thurloe 3:249 et seq.
 6. Br. Mus. Add. Mss. 124:29.
 7. Immediately after the arrival of the fleet, the soldiers had been put on shore to be quartered and fed by the Barbadians. This was common practice.
 8. Thurloe 3:249 et seq.
 9. Thurloe 3:754; Penn 2:46.
10. Venables App. 121; Thurloe 4:28.
11. Andrews 2:8, 9 note 2.
12. I. S. 20.

9

French
Prisoner

In 1660, France claimed that she had taken and settled the island of St. Lucia in 1640 and had held it continuously since then, without British opposition. St. Lucia lay adjacent to and northwest of Barbados. France based her claim on a 1627 voyage of settlement. Britain insisted that she, herself, had discovered St. Lucia in 1593 and established settlements there in 1605, 1626, 1638 and 1640.

France set forth that this British claim was magnified out of all proportion. The British, they said, may have tried to settle St. Lucia, but because of the fierceness of the cannibals on the island, they were not able to settle permanently any of these times, as they claimed.

The natives indeed were a savage lot. "They went stark naked and painted their bodies with red ocher and drew a vermillion stroke from their ears to their noses."[1] The first group sent there by the British was a small band of prisoners, which was completely annihilated.

In 1640, the same year that the French placed a lasting settlement on St. Lucia, Captain Philip Bell had received permission from the British Privy Council to take one hundred forty settlers and the necessary provisions to the island of St. Lucia to start a settlement. This venture did not succeed, as previous ones had not. After one year, Bell and his followers retreated to Barbados.

France pointed out that she was able to handle the natives and, that after 1640, she had held St. Lucia for twenty years. Britain argued that during this same twenty year period her people were engaged in civil war, and it was not until 1660, when Charles II had come to the throne to replace the Cromwellian Commonwealth, that she could again assert her claim over St. Lucia.

To this end, in 1660, Charles II granted his loyal supporter, Lord

Francis Willoughby, who had returned to power as Governor of Barbados, a patent for St. Lucia with half of the profits taken from the venture to go to Willoughby for seven years.[2] Willoughby's next move was to make arrangements to take over from the French, forcibly of course, and to start making some profits. Colonel Lewis Morris and some associates were enlisted in the endeavor.

First Colonel Morris got together with Amiwatta Baba, native chief proprietor of the Caribbe Islands, and three other natives. He arranged to give the four chiefs some money to quiet any title they might claim to St. Lucia, thus hoping to have them on his side when the invasion took place.[3] This contract with the natives was secretly made in 1663.

In 1664 the year after Morris had made his contract with Amiwatta Baba, a British invasion of St. Lucia was undertaken, supported by six hundred Caribbe Indians in their canoes. The British were welcomed by the natives and the island was easily captured. All French were dispossessed of their property. Morris and his associates took control, and they installed a substantial settlement of one thousand persons on St. Lucia.[4]

France claimed that this was a deceitful and vicious plan to deprive France of what was justly hers. She claimed that Governor Willoughby did not come to the island himself to assert the British claim, implying that the invasion was a private enterprise by Lewis Morris and his associates and was not done in Britain's interest.

France also argued that the contract negotiated by Morris with the native chiefs was fallacious. France asserted that Morris got the chiefs drunk and made some sort of agreement with them. France went on to show that, with full knowledge of Britain, these chiefs earlier had relinquished all claims to the island of St. Lucia in favor of France, and therefore had nothing to pass on to the British. The French stated that there was no mention in the British agreement with the natives of any price paid for the island, and the sale concocted by Morris was a fraud.

In summary, France said that "The fruit of drunkenness of four savages and dishonesty of purchasers is therefore only fit to shew the little confidence people in the Caribbe Islands as well as in England had in all their pretended claims for St. Lucia."[5]

Morris and his group put every possible effort back of the colonization of St. Lucia, but by the end of the first year, matters were not going well. There were frequent raids on the settlement by the ferocious native savages. The British settlers lived every moment in fear.

Eventually sickness struck the colony and there was agitation to leave the island. After being in possession of St. Lucia about eighteen months, the British were again obliged to return to Barbados. No sooner had the British left, than the French returned, but when the British heard that the French were back on the island, they launched a series of raids. Within two months after the British had left, the French were complaining of British piracy at St. Lucia. Lewis Morris later would be charged with one of these acts of piracy.

This was the status of St. Lucia in 1666 when France decided to enter the war already going on between Britain and Holland. The French and British had long since jointly occupied St. Christopher Island—each governed one half of it. When war was declared, the British on St. Christopher were the first to attack, but through some miscalculation, perhaps treason, they were defeated. Eight thousand British on the island were taken prisoner and shipped away, and all British property was seized.

A temporary peace was signed in July, 1667. Five months later three hundred British prisoners were released by the French. But the French refused to give back the British half of the island, apparently waiting for final peace terms to be negotiated and signed in Europe. The Governor of Barbados wrote to the Secretary of State that something should be done to negotiate with the French for the return of the British part of the island. The home government suggested Colonel Lewis Morris as the appropriate intermediary for these negotiations, but the governor did not act upon this suggestion.[6]

In May, 1668, almost a year after the temporary peace, the final treaty was signed at Aix-la-Chappelle. Strangely, it mentioned nothing about St. Lucia or St. Christopher—serving as further excuse for the French to delay the return of the British part of St. Christopher.

Finally, Charles II requested of the Barbadian governor that Colonel Lewis Morris try to negotiate the matter. Thus, on June 28, 1668, Colonel Simon Lambarte wrote to the King: "in obedience to his Majesty's commission, Colonel Morris, Colonel Robert Hopper and myself agree to demand the English part of St. Christopher."[7] These negotiations failed.

Almost a year and a half had passed since the cease fire, and St.

Christopher was still completely in the hands of the French. The Governor of Barbados was so incensed by the delays that he asked the King to give his authorization to continue the war on a privateering basis. The King did give his authority in the following words, "and empowering him [the Governor] to commission what ever persons he thought good to be partners with his Majesty in the plunder, they finding victals, wear and tear." This was unmistakable permission to continue the war.

Now privateering again became the order of the day. During this period, Colonel Morris was captured by the French and imprisoned. The charge lodged against Morris was: "for depredations by sea before and after the war," meaning before and after July 21, 1667,[8] which was the date when a temporary peace was signed.

Shortly after Morris was imprisoned, one of his lieutenants, in one of Morris' ships, captured a large French vessel at St. Lucia and brought her into port at Barbados. This would compound Morris' difficulties.

From his prison cell, Morris sent word of his capture to the Governor at Barbados through two negroes. He urged that the Governor enter negotiations for his release. His message also urged the Governor to withhold releasing any more French prisoners accused of piracy, until he was released. The Governor failed in his attempt to negotiate Morris' release, and he wrote to England to enlist the help of the Secretary of State. The Governor, however, expressed his opinion that unless Morris, through his lieutenant, returned the French ship taken at St. Lucia, it might be difficult to get him out of prison.[9]

Morris claimed to his captors that he was innocent. He said that he was now a Quaker, and as such, would not have participated in the deeds of which he was accused. To the Governor, Morris communicated that he was being held "in a strang land," by a "man who had hopes of enriching himselfe" thereby.[10] The fact that Morris said that he was being held in a strange land would suggest that it was at a place unfamiliar to him, somewhere in the Caribbean.

Sometime around midyear 1670 Colonel Lewis Morris was set free. He returned home to Barbados and wrote Lord Arlington, Secretary of State, thanking him for help in obtaining his release.

When Lewis Morris came out of prison, peace between Spain, Holland and France had been made, and the island war had been forgotten by most everyone—but not by Lewis Morris.

---

1. America 377.
2. Hague 1 et seq.
3. Bolton 2:286.
4. Newton-West Indies 243.
5. Hague 1 et seq.
6. CO Col. Papers Vol. XXII #60; CSPC 1661–1668:556, 562.
7. CO Col. Papers Vol. XXII #129, 129I, 129II; CSPC 1661–1668:579.
8. CO Col. Papers Vol. XXIV #79, 80; CSPC 1669–1674: 37.
9. Ibid.
10. Co Col. Papers Vol. XXVII #36; CSPC 1669–1674:262.

10

New York Merchant

By 1663, Barbados, one of Britain's strongholds in the Caribbean, was in a depression. Samuel Argall's northern route from England to the western world across the north Atlantic was becoming popular, and Barbados was no longer a hub of western commerce. The secret of sugar refining had become known in other parts, and there was a great migration away from Barbados to land not held at such a premium. In despair, the Governor of Barbados wrote to the King that "Barbados is decaying fast."[1]

These were some of the economic reasons why Colonel Morris now longed to move away from Barbados—and his opportunity was soon to come. In 1663, the British were making immediate plans to seize New York and New Jersey, then occupied by the Dutch, illegally according to the British. Britain based her North American claim on John Cabot's voyage in 1497. The Dutch based their claim on Henry Hudson's voyage of 1609.

Actual permanent British and Dutch colonization in what is now the United States, however, did not commence until early in the 1600s. While the British were colonizing Virginia, Maryland, and New England, beginning in 1607, the Dutch were settling in New York, New Jersey and Delaware, beginning in 1610. The pattern was much like it had been in the West Indies, where each European power seized some land, then tried to hold onto it while asserting its claim.

Then, on March 12, 1664, Charles II granted to his brother James, Duke of York, all of the land from the Connecticut River to Delaware Bay, including off shore islands, plus Maine east of the Kennebec River.

Colonel Richard Nicolls was chosen to enforce the King's Grant in the Dutch held area, mainly New York and New Jersey, lying between the two British colonies of Connecticut and Maryland. With four ships and 450 foot soldiers, some say as few as 300, Colonel Nicolls arrived off New Amsterdam in August, 1664. After several exchanges of letters from ship to shore, Governor Peter Stuyvesant capitulated, whereupon Nicolls took over as Governor from Peter Stuyvesant and renamed New Amsterdam, New York, after James, Duke of York.

Soon after his arrival, Nicolls began encouraging trade, and issuing patents for land in New York and in New Jersey. The two principal grants in New Jersey were the Monmouth Patent issued in 1664 and the Elizabethtown Patent issued in 1665.

British occupation of New York and New Jersey was the opportunity for which Colonel Lewis Morris was waiting. He soon established his younger brother, Richard Morris, in New York to operate a branch of his vast sugar, shipping and trading enterprise already firmly established in the West Indies. This was preparatory to the Colonel's own permanent removal to New York.

As early as 1666, Colonel Lewis Morris and Richard Morris, the latter often referred to as Captain Richard Morris, were involved in New York over the Customs duty on 13,370 pounds of sugar.[2]

By 1668, Colonel Lewis Morris had purchased a two hundred and fifty margen estate (about 500 acres) in the Bronx, on the Westchester side of the Harlem River, just northwest of what is now Randalls Island. The Colonel named his new estate "Morrisania."

The property previously had been called "Bronx Land," for Jonas Bronx who acquired it from the Indians, and started building a house near the water's edge in 1639. Sometime after Jonas Bronx' death, the property was sold by his heirs for 2,000 guilders in beaver skins. It then passed through several hands to Samuel Edsall, who on June 4, 1668, sold the property to Colonel Lewis Morris.[3]

The Colonel, acting through his brother Richard, acquired additional large land tracts in and about New York City, some by grant and some by purchase from original grantees.[4] The Colonel's Long Island holdings were centered about a place known as Matinecock, or Oyster Bay. There, as early as 1670, he purchased 1,000 acres including Matinecock Point, and in 1671, he bought Centre, or "Hog" Island, at the mouth of Oyster Bay. One grant at Oyster Bay, for 1,054 acres, was applied for as late as 1683.

PLATE 4

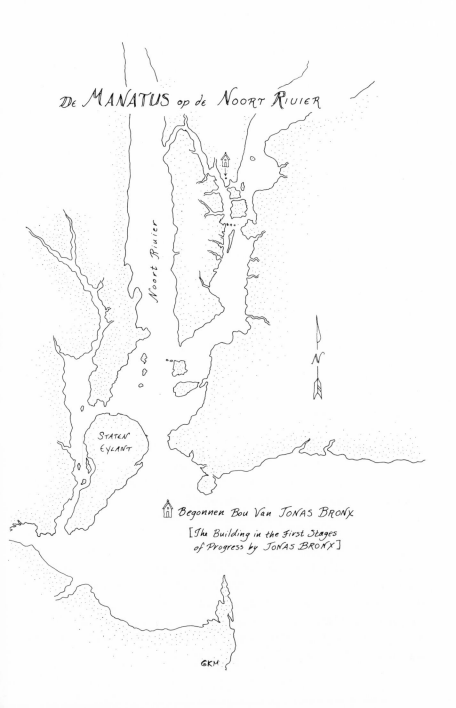

De *MANATUS* op de *NOORT RIVIER*

Noort Rivier

N

STATEN EYLANT

🏠 Begonnen Bou Van JONAS BRONX

[The Building in the First Stages of Progress by JONAS BRONX]

GKM

The Colonel also acquired holdings in New Jersey on the Delaware River where, in 1672, he and his brother, Richard, were granted 1,000 acres in the Finn's Point, Salem Cove area, across from New Castle. This grant was made three years prior to any other recorded English grant in West Jersey.[5]

Although there is no evidence that Colonel Morris used his properties for other than honorable purposes, the record would not be complete unless it was pointed out that Oyster Bay, in those days, was a haven for smugglers bent on escaping a ten percent customs duty on shipping levied at New York.[6]

According to the minutes of the Common Council of the City of New York, it was reported that "Severall Quantities of fflower are dayly imported into this citty for sale and Transportation perticulerly for by Coll. Lewis Morris [and said flour is] ordered siezed as contrary to law."[7]

Colonel Morris and his brother, Captain Richard, were often in the New York courts defending their actions as merchants. The Colonel was very accomplished at the law, having served on the Governing Council of Barbados for many years, during which time that body also acted as the highest court of the island. He frequently appeared in New York courts and some of his arguments on jurisdiction and points of law are still preserved.[8] Richard Morris also appeared often in New York courts as "atturney" for Colonel Lewis Morris and others.[9]

Notwithstanding his many other activities, Colonel Lewis Morris' main interest was the growing, refining and shipping of sugar products. One year alone he shipped from his vast West Indian plantations 444,712 pounds of sugar in various forms—muscovado, clayed sugar, refined sugar, also rum and molasses.[10] London and New York were his principal markets.[11]

During this period, the Colonel was one of the largest users of the New York dock facilities and he was heavily taxed for a dock expansion program instituted in 1668. A New York tax notice stated, "it has been lately ordered that all and every person that trades at New York pay for a new Dock proportionately to the value of his property." Colonel Lewis Morris' port evaluation for this purpose was established at £1,000.[12]

On June 28, 1668, about the time the New York dock tax assessment was being made, and only three weeks after Colonel Morris purchased

Morrisania, he was back in Barbados, consenting to negotiate with the French regarding the postwar return of the British half of St. Christopher Island, during which period he was captured by the French and imprisoned.

---

1. Co Col. Papers Vol. XVII #89; CSPC 1661–1668:167.
2. NAR 6:135, 257, 258.
3. Riker 260, 261, 262, 431, 432; Bolton 2:283.
4. Oyster Bay 1:117, 172, 176, 182, 183, 309; Land Papers 2:127; Thompson 2:439.
5. Salem Deed Book B:10, 86, 113; 1 NJA 21:565, 566; Riker 262.
6. Cooks 10.
7. Council 1:95.
8. NY Col. Mss. 25 et seq., indexed p. 42; ibid 137, indexed p. 47; Riker 431–441.
9. NAR 6:302.
10. Morris 1677 Account.
11. NY Col. Mss. 25, indexed p. 42.
12. Council 1:25, 26.

11

Dutch Adversary

When Richard Morris heard of the Colonel's imprisonment in the West Indies, he hurried back to Barbados to assist in gaining his brother's freedom.

While in Barbados, Richard married Sarah Poole. The ceremony took place August 17, 1669, in St. Michael's Anglican Church. Whether either Richard or Sarah previously had been married is not known. Richard was about fifty-three. Sarah was referred to as "a young woman in the prime of life," which would suggest that she was younger than he.[1]

As to Sarah Poole's ancestry, her grandson, Robert Hunter Morris, did not know what it was, though he made it his business to try to find out. He was unsuccessful—noting that "from whom she is descended we are totally ignorant."[2]

On August 10, 1670, five days before Richard and Sarah Morris' first anniversary, and shortly after the Colonel's release from his French prison, the Colonel and Richard entered into a written agreement in which it was stipulated that two thirds of all real estate in the name of Richard Morris belonged to the Colonel. The agreement further provided that if either of them should die without issue, the survivor, or issue of the survivor, shall take the estate of the other.[3] Soon thereafter Richard returned to New York with his bride, and they moved into "Morrisania."

The Colonel was not without another home in which to reside while in New York. He had a house located one block north of Pearl Street. It was on the south side of Bridge Street, the second house from the corner of what is now Whitehall and Bridge Streets.[4] Whitehall was then called "The Marketfield," and was rather wide at that point

59

creating almost a park effect between the houses and the southeast bastion of Fort James.

Next door to Colonel Morris, on the corner of Bridge and White-hall, lived Cornelius Steenwyck, who was one of the principal merchants of New York, dealing mainly in tobacco, salt and slaves.[5] He was said to have been one of the richest men in town. Steenwyck became a very close friend of the Colonel, and they were to have many business dealings as the years went on.

On October 15, 1671, a little over a year after the date of the Colonel's and Richard's survival agreement, a son was born to Richard and Sarah Morris. They named the child, Lewis, in honor of his uncle, the colonel.

Less than a year later tragedy struck. In July 1672, Sarah Morris died. A week later Richard died.[6] Walter Webley, the Colonel's brother-in-law, who was then living in New York, died about the same time, preceded in death by his wife (sister of Colonel and Richard Morris) said to be named Mary.[7] The cause of these sudden deaths is not known, but they must have been due to some communicable disease or to an accident, in order for so many to be stricken so fast.

Richard and Sarah Morris were survived by young Lewis Morris, who was less than a year old. Walter Webley and his wife Mary, were survived by sons Edward and Walter, Jr., the latter about forty, and living in Harlem just across from Morrisania.[8]

The Colonel was in Barbados when these multiple deaths took place, and the infant Lewis temporarily was taken into the home of Walter Webley, Jr. Webley also took over Richard's former duties of caring for the Colonel's New York shipping and sugar interests.

A short time before Richard Morris' death, Governor Lovelace had warned the citizens of New York to assume a posture of defense against a possible attempt by the Dutch to retake New York. "Captain Richard Morris"[9] had been appointed commissioner to receive sub-scriptions to repair Fort James, but Richard died not long thereafter, without completing his task.

At the time of Richard Morris' death, there was serving in New York an English army officer who in time would play an important role in colonial American history. His name was Edmund Andros. Andros had been in America as early as 1666, as an army major, where he spent two years before returning to England, later being assigned to

PLATE 5

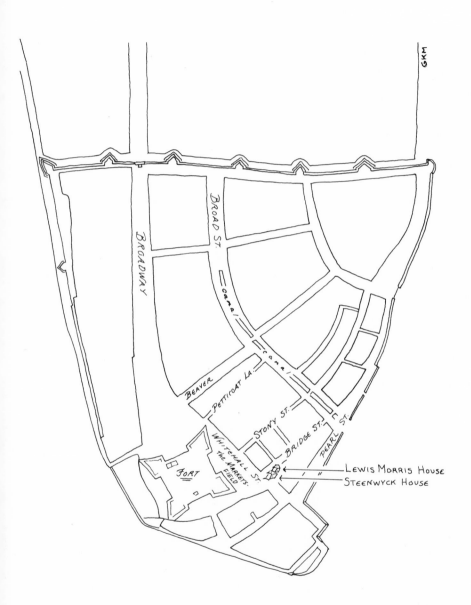

GKM

BROADWAY

BROAD ST.

canal

canal

BEAVER

PETTICOAT LA.

STONY ST.

BRIDGE ST.

E ST.

PEARL ST.

WHITEHALL ST.

THE MARKETS FIELD

FORT

LEWIS MORRIS HOUSE
STEENWYCK HOUSE

Barbados where he was in charge of all military forces.[10] Whether it was in America or in Barbados that Colonel Lewis Morris and Major Edmund Andros met, is not known. However, a firm friendship developed between these two men, which would be evident many times in the years to come.

The high place held by Andros in the New York provincial government, as early as 1672, is illustrated by his signature on the document which appointed administrators for the estate of Richard Morris. Such a responsibility was the accustomed privilege of the Governor.[11]

After signing the document of administration, Andros appointed, as administrators of Richard's estate, Captain Matthias Nicoll, mayor of New York (no relative of the former Governor Colonel Richard Nicolls); Captain Thomas Delavall, former mayor of New York; Captain Cornelius Steenwyck on the governing Council of New York Province; Captain John Berry, acting governor of New Jersey; and Thomas Gibbs, Sheriff of New York.

These men were appointed not only because of their high offices, but because they were also old friends of the Morris family. Captain Berry was from Barbados, and had come to America in 1669.[12] Captain Thomas Delavall was a neighbor in Westchester and believed to have been, formerly, a Barbadian.[13] Captain Cornelius Steenwyck was a next door neighbor in New York City.[14] Matthias Nicoll was Richard's "dear friend."[15] The only administrator not identified as a friend was Thomas Gibbs, the sheriff.[16]

As predicted by Governor Lovelace, war was declared by England against Holland in March 1673. This time it was the British and French against the Dutch. As soon as it was learned that a state of war existed, Walter Webley, Jr., scurried to get all of the valuables of Colonel Lewis and Captain Richard Morris loaded onto one or more of the Colonel's vessels, the Colonel being in Barbados at the time.[17] A shipload was taken to New Haven, which had never been under Dutch control.[18] It is believed that another cargo was taken to New Jersey.

The Dutch invasion came a few months later. Some say that the defenders fought four hours until all ammunition ran out, and then surrendered. At any rate, it was not a difficult victory for the Dutch, and they retook possession of New York on July 30, 1673.

Hearing of the invasion, Colonel Morris hurried back to America. He did not try to come into New York harbor, but went directly to New

Jersey. After all, he had been one of the English merchants who had taken over much of the New York trade after the Dutch were forced to give up the government of New York nine years earlier. He was in danger of being taken into custody for alleged acts against the Dutch, some probably based on fact and some not.[19]

Upon his arrival in New Jersey, the Colonel learned that, on the very day that the Mayor of New York "delivered [to the Dutch] his gown and cloak with the city seal and mace," Walter Webley, Jr., had been summoned to testify in New York.[20] The Dutch governing council asked Webley to prove that the goods shipped from Barbados and in his possession (probably sugar products in warehouses, etc.) belonged to him. If the merchandise would be found to belong not to him but to Webley's employer and uncle, Colonel Lewis Morris, it was to be confiscated.

All the Colonel's property and merchandise that could be found was seized soon thereafter to support the Dutch occupation. Colonel Anthony Colve, the new Dutch Governor, even confiscated and sold slaves belonging to the Colonel and found living at Morrisania.[21]

Learning that everything that could be identified as his had been taken, Colonel Morris wrote Governor Colve, asking that, if nothing else, he be granted Morrisania for the benefit of the orphaned child, Lewis, and that he be made guardian of the child.[22] At least he could salvage something that way. Furthermore, he had an undisclosed two-thirds interest in Richard's real property.

The Colonel had reason to hope that this request would be granted inasmuch as Cornelius Steenwyck, his friend and neighbor, had been retained by Colve on the Dutch Governor's council. Things might have gone well if the Governor had not found out that Walter Webley, Jr., had hidden much of the Morris valuables. As a result of this discovery, Governor Colve refused the Colonel's request for guardianship unless the property was returned.

The Colonel, still in New Jersey, wrote to the Governor again asking that a pass be granted Walter Webley, Jr., who had since escaped to Jersey, so that Webley could return to New York to gather together plate, etc., so as to make an inventory of it for Governor Colve. In reply, Governor Colve granted the pass to Webley and promised the guardianship to the Colonel as soon as all of the valuables were returned.[23]

When Webley arrived back in New York, he gathered together some of the plate and other valuables held at his house and at the house of Thomas Delavall, who lived just north of Morrisania on Mill Creek, but Webley did not go to New Haven to recover that portion of the hidden treasure.

An inventory was taken of the part recovered by Webley, and the Dutch appointed new administrators of Richard's estate. They were Messrs. John Lawrence, an English gentleman; Stephanus van Cortland, a Dutch gentleman; and Walter Webley, Jr. These men also were made guardians of the child, Lewis, which was a blow to the Colonel.[24]

The new administrators soon found out, which Webley already knew, that all of the valuables had not been recovered; this further complicated matters. To the end of gathering together all of the treasure, Colonel Morris was given a pass from Governor Colve to go in search of it, "on condition that he attempt nothing to its [the Dutch government's] prejudice during his sojourn."[25]

When the Colonel found so little of the hidden valuables at New Haven, he became suspicious that looting had taken place, yet he knew Colve would not believe such a story. The Colonel, therefore, came back only as far as Shelter Island, where he again wrote to Governor Colve regarding the persecution of those who appeared not to submit wholly to the Dutch. Although his appeal was a general one, he surely was speaking for himself, and of the suspicion with which the Dutch must have regarded his inability to produce the valuables.

In response to the Colonel's letter, Governor Colve sent Cornelius Steenwyck, the Colonel's friend, to Shelter Island, located between the two arms of the eastern end of Long Island, to hear the Colonel's complaint.[26] Sylvester or Shelter Island was owned by Nathaniel Sylvester, a former Barbados planter, Quaker, and dear friend of the Colonel.

Still concerned about coming to New York, even after Steenwyck's visit, the Colonel wrote Governor Colve stating that he had gone to Oyster Bay (previously noted as a Morris holding) and to New Haven to pick up "some of the missing estate," and that he would like to bring what he had found at New Haven, either to Oyster Bay, Sylvester Island or New York "with the sloop belonging to my cousin's plantation."[27]

Whether the Colonel ever entered New York during Dutch occupation or ever turned over any plate or jewels to Colve has not been determined. It is known that the Dutch did not make the Colonel guardian of the infant Lewis' estate but gave the appointment to Walter Webley, Jr. The Colonel resented this and he felt that Webley had willfully and feloniously appropriated some of the valuables for his own use and had secured the appointment of himself as guardian and administrator in the Colonel's stead.

On February 9, 1674, peace was signed with the Dutch, at Westminster (without the necessity of British reinvasion at New York), which provided for the return of New York, New Jersey, etc. to Britain.

Nearly a month after the signing of the peace treaty, the Dutch made a change of guardianship of the infant, Lewis Morris. Two new guardians were appointed, yet Walter Webley, Jr., remained as one of the three.

Seven months after the peace had been concluded, and long after the peace news had reached America, the Dutch were still nominating officers in New Jersey. It was not until October 31, 1674, almost nine months after peace had been signed, that New York was actually turned over to Edmund Andros, the new British Governor. All this time, Colonel Lewis Morris was hovering around the periphery of New York. It had been a long, strenuous and costly two years since his brother's death.[28]

---

1. Stillwell 4:15.
2. Morris RHM 1763 Corres.
3. Riker 262.
4. Valentine 1853:239; Bolton 2:293 line 4.
5. Stokes 2:264; DAB 17:558.
6. Stokes 4:285.
7. NYD 2:595; Morris RHM 1763 Corres.
8. Stillwell 4:21, 23; GMNJ 26:74.
9. Stokes 4:285.
10. Whitmore 13.
11. NY Wills 1:25.
12. CO Col. Entry Bk. XI p.98–102; CSPC 1661–1668:450, 451, 453, 456, 457, 469; NYG&BR Apr. 1884:50; PNJHS (NS) 14:402, 404.
13. CSPC 1660–1674:546.
14. PNJHS Oct. 1952:252; Stokes 2:264.
15. Stillwell 4:15.
16. Council 8:145; Stillwell 4:15.
17. Bolton 2:231 lines 20–23.

18. NYD 2:664; Stillwell 4:17.
19. Analytical Index Oct. 7, 1667.
20. NAR 6:399.
21. NY Col. Mss. 23:20–28, indexed 84.
22. NYD 2:637.
23. Ibid: 617, 637.
24. Ibid: 650, 651; Stillwell 4:17.
25. 1 NJA 1:134.
26. Brodhead 2:227, 228.
27. NYD 2:664. The identity of the Colonel's cousin at New Haven is not known. At the time, however, there was a family of Morrises living there. *East Haven Register*, New Haven, 1824 (p.162); *Genealogy of the Morris Family of Connecticut* by Lucy Ann Morris Carhart, New York, 1911; *History of East Haven* by Sarah E. Hughes, New Haven, 1908; *New England Historical and Genealogical Register* 71:5.
28. A provocative aftermath to the whole matter of the personal effects taken from New York by Walter Webley, Jr., is found in a published account in the Historical Collections of New Jersey by Barber and Howe. It relates that in 1670 young Lewis Morris, son of Thomas of Barbados, with the aid of Colonel Lewis Morris, bought a parcel of land in Monmouth County, New Jersey, from the Indians for a barrel of cider.

Young Lewis Morris moved onto the land shortly before the Dutch occupation, whereupon all of the Indians on the property moved back to Crosswicks and Cranberry except one "Indian Will," who was allowed to stay and dwell in a wigwam between Tinton Falls and Swimming River. One day, sometime after the Dutch had left, Indian Will, while eating breakfast of suppawn (mush) and milk, was observed using a silver spoon. Mr. Thomas Eaton, of what is now Eatontown, New Jersey, told Indian Will, his friend, that he would give him a red cloak and a cocked hat if he would tell where he found the spoon. It seems that Indian Will was soon wearing the red cloak and cocked hat and Mr. Eaton suddenly became rich.

Indian Will was also a friend of Derrick Longstreet and one time showed Longstreet some silver money. Longstreet asked Will to give it to him, but Will refused. Will did, however, give Longstreet some yellow money he had found, which the Indian thought worthless. This made Longstreet rich. Stillwell 4:15.

12

New Jersey
Industrialist

Newly appointed British Governor of New York, Edmund Andros, and returning British Governor of New Jersey, Philip Carteret, arrived in New York from England on the same boat on the last day of October 1674, to take over from the Dutch who had held New York and New Jersey since July 30, 1673, a period of fifteen months.

Soon after his arrival in New York, Governor Andros was presented with a petition on behalf of Colonel Lewis Morris. It asked that the Colonel be granted additional lands adjacent to Morrisania because he had sustained such great losses as a result of the Dutch occupation. The petition was prepared by Walter Webley, Jr., indicating some sort of reconciliation with his uncle, the Colonel.[1]

In response to the petition, Andros granted 1,420 acres to Colonel Morris adjoining his 500 acres already held at Morrisania. With this new grant, Morrisania consisted of 1,920 acres, and embraced a very substantial part of what is now the Borough of the Bronx, New York City. For the entire tract, the grant stated that the Colonel was to pay "yearly and every year as quitt rent to his Royal Highness five bushels of good winter wheat."[2] In days to come, Andros would be censured by His Royal Highness, the Duke of York, for these non-revenue producing grants to friends.

Colonel Morris moved into Morrisania when he arrived back in New York rather than into his downtown New York house on Bridge Street, where he had resided while Richard occupied Morrisania.

No sooner had the Colonel become well reestablished at Morrisania, than he again turned his attentions to business, this time in New Jersey. There, the Colonel had connections that were not in the least inferior to his connections in New York. Governor Philip Carteret of New Jersey was a friend, dating back several years.

Captain John Berry, deputy governor under Carteret, and acting governor when Philip Carteret went to England prior to the Dutch invasion, was from Barbados and a previously identified friend of the Colonel.

William Sandford, also from Barbados, was on the Governing Council of New Jersey, coming to America in 1668. He was a long time friend of Colonel Morris, having served with him on the Governing Council of Barbados from 1656 through 1659.[3]

James Bollen, Secretary to the government of New Jersey, was not only a friend, but had several financial arrangements with Colonel Morris dating back as far as January 1668, when Bollen borrowed "sewant," or wampum money, from the Colonel.[4]

It was under these favorable conditions of government that Colonel Morris decided to invest heavily in Jersey enterprise. On December 29, 1675, he purchased one half interest in a bog iron property located in what is now Monmouth County, New Jersey, in an area called Hockhockson Swamp.[5]

The discovery site was situated in the vicinity of a farm near the present Tinton Falls, New Jersey, owned by the Colonel and the residence of the Colonel's ward, teen-aged Lewis Morris, "son of Thomas of Barbados" said to be a "relation." Lewis had been raised "from infancy"[6] by the Colonel. (This Lewis Morris, son of Thomas, should not be confused with the two year old Lewis Morris, son of the Colonel's deceased brother, Richard, both of whom were wards of the Colonel.)

It is very probable that the Hockhockson ore deposit was discovered in 1673 or 1674 and that the Colonel was interested in the project from its early development. The Colonel's purchase agreement with James Grover in December 1675 for one half interest in the ore property mentioned a "first agreement," which dated back to August 24, 1674, when Grover and his two partners, Richard Hartshorne and John Bowne, purchased the ore property from the Indians.[7] This was during the Dutch occupation and while the Colonel was persona non grata with the Dutch.

In December 1674, three months after purchase from the Indians, a loan was made to Grover by Colonel Morris' friend, Cornelius Steenwyck, who advanced James Grover £100 on a two year basis to help finance the iron venture—Grover pledging one-fourth interest in the mine as security for the loan.[8]

The £100 loan went quickly, and at the end of the first year Grover needed more money. This forced him to offer for sale one-half interest in the mine. Colonel Lewis Morris was now present to buy a one-half, or "moiety" interest—later taking over the Steenwyck loan, which gave him ownership of three-fourths of the ore property.[9]

Grover must, finally, have realized that he was engulfed in an undertaking not suited to a man of modest means. John Winthrop, son of the governor of Massachusetts Colony, had poured £10,000 into his Braintree, Mass. iron works, and had abandoned it as too costly. Yet, wealthy as the Colonel was, he did not go into the iron mining business blindly. One month and twenty days before he had purchased one half interest in the ore property from Grover, Morris had secured from his friendly connections in New Jersey, some extremely favorable land concessions, not to be officially issued and published until a year and a half later. During this intervening period the Colonel would greatly increase his holdings by grant from the friendly New York and New Jersey governments of Edmund Andros and Philip Carteret.

The concessions granted to Morris specified, among other things, "That the land and those that worked at the Iron Works bee rate free for a tearme of seven years... That the said Land bee Rent free for five years... That the Workmen bee free from Arrest for Debt... That they shall be free from pressing, mustering, Watching and Trayning [military service]...."[10]

As soon as Colonel Morris made his arrangements with the New Jersey government and closed his purchase for one-half interest from Grover, he set about acquiring more properties containing ore deposits.

In addition to the discovery property, surveyed out at 3,840 acres (3,540 plus 300 for roads), the New Jersey government granted Morris 1,500 acres northwest of the discovery acreage and 500 acres to the east of the discovery property.[11] He also purchased several adjoining pieces from original grantees.[12] Further, Morris was granted exclusive rights to dig ore in a vastly larger area from "ye southeast branch of ye Raritan River,"[13] now South River, to the ocean.

Later, when the concession relative to the deferment of quitrents
ran out, Morris was able to get his back quitrents completely erased
and a new rate set at one quart of spring water per year, which was not
much of an increase over nothing.[14]

Morris did not wait for the final issuing of the concessions to start
operating the iron works. On May 5, 1676, within five months of the
purchase from Grover, the books of "Tinton Iron Works" were
opened.[15] The first three items entered in the books symbolized the life
style at Tinton, and the hard work that lay ahead. The entries were:

1676, May 5th	7 iron spades	£3:10:0
	1 Barrel Beefe	2:00:0
	3 Ankers Rum	9:00:0

James Grover and Samuel Leonard (the latter coming to Jersey
with his father Henry Leonard Sr. from Taunton, Massachusetts, to
provide the Grover group their iron working knowledge) were sent to
the New Haven Iron Works in Connecticut to purchase cast parts and
bar iron from which to forge other parts.

Leather was purchased for a bellows. A blast furnace was built and a
number of men were hired. There was activity on all fronts. At first
there was only one chafry, or forge hammer, at the works but this was
later increased to two.

It took about 2,000 acres of timber, made into charcoal, to supply
one furnace for a year. Charcoal, at Tinton, was made from pine logs
seven to twelve inches in diameter, which was about a ten year stand or
growth. This cycle called for about 20,000 acres to keep a furnace running, which was more land than the Colonel owned. His acreage was
only about 6,000 acres, much of it without timber. However, before
the Colonel ran out of acreage he was able to get a 21-year lease from
the New Jersey government "in appreciation for service."[16] This permitted him to cut timber and pine trees, and to gather and produce
pitch, rosin and turpentine outside of his own holdings.

A 1679 published account tells something of the Colonel Lewis
Morris installations and of Shrewsbury Town in which the works was
located: "Shrewsbury, A Town in the Province lyes without Sandy-
point [Sandy Hook] and hath the farthest plantation to the Southward
[nothing south of it in New Jersey along the coast until possibly Cape
May]. It is situate on the [south] side of a River [Navesink and Swim-

PLATE 6

ming Rivers] not far from its entrance, and extends up into the Land a little distant from the said River about eight miles near unto Colonel Morice his Iron Mill and Plantation. [Townships in Monmouth County were not established until 1693 and at this early date the boundary of one town ran to the boundary of another].

"There is within its jurisdiction Colonel Morice, his Mannour, being [about six] thousand acres, wherein are his iron Mills, his Mannours, and diverse other buildings for his servants and dependents there, together with 60 or 70 negroes, about the Mill and Husbandries, in that plantation.

"There are diverse out plantations, accounted to belong to the juris-diction of the Town, some in the Necks of Land by the Sea Side others within land, and towards Middletown bounds, and others to the northside of the River below Collonel Morice his Iron Mills: The computation of Acres taken up by the Town may be 10,000 Acres, and what is taken up by Collonel Morice and other out-plantations, 20,000 Acres, the number of families in the Town are 80 and of Inhabitants, Men, Women and Children 400."[17]

Colonel Morris did not come to live in New Jersey when he bought the iron works. He still maintained his residence in New York at Morrisania. In fact, until the year 1679, he kept his old residence in Barbados.[18]

The iron works was not the Colonel's main business enterprise. He had his vast sugar plantations in the West Indies and his large merchant shipping interests in New York. The iron works did, how-ever, play an important part in the whole complex of his activities. Bar iron was almost as good as gold and accepted as a medium of exchange throughout the world. Wampum was accepted mainly in local trade and even beaver skins had their limitations as a medium of exchange. Iron was not perishable. It took up little room aboard ship. It made perfect ballast, and it was much in demand.

A Tinton Iron Works ledger and day book from 1675 to 1683 shows that the works was in full operation at least for that period. As revealed in the ledger and day book, total expenditures for equipment, salaries, etc., to that date, amounted to £8,680. The works, however, seems to have been in operation beyond 1683, for a Tinton Iron Works accounts receivable sheet still exists for the date October 8, 1687, totaling £112:10:6.[19] Not much is known of the works beyond 1687 except that there is evidence that it was still in operation as late as 1708.[20]

The ten buildings in the main complex at the iron works are shown in a contemporary sketch perspective with windows and roofs. It is attributed to Robert Vauquellin, Surveyor General for the province from 1664 to 1681. The sketch is labeled "Tinton Manor Colonel Lewis Moriss." The buildings lie close to the falls on "Falles Creek" or "Mill Creek," now known as Pine Brook, which is a branch of Swimming River. Buildings are shown on all four corners of what is now the junction of Sycamore Avenue and Tinton Avenue in the Borough of Tinton Falls.[21]

1. NY Col. Mss. 24:2, indexed p. 31.
2. Bolton 2:289.
3. Journal Aug. 1943:176; NYG&BR Apr. 1884:49; 1NJA 2:314; Whitehead 116.
4. Tinton: Ledger.
5. Tinton: Dec. 29, 1675, Bill of Sale. The swamp was called "Hockoceung" by the Indians in their deeds to the white man. Stillwell 3:254, 255.
6. Tinton: 3.30.1688 and 4.15.1689 Deeds; Morris: 4.24.1689 Release; Morris: RHM 6.7.1763 Letter.
7. Tinton: Dec. 29, 1675 Bill of Sale; East Jersey Deeds Bk. 1, p. 68; Stillwell 3:254.
8. Tinton: Dec. 8, 1674 Agreement.
9. Morris: July 21, 1677 Assignment.
10. Tinton: May 1, 1677 Concessions.
11. 1,500 acre tract, Morris: Oct. 4, 1676 Randall Huitt Purchase; Tinton: Oct. 27, 1676 Request for Survey; Miller 9; Morris: Survey map for 1,500 acres, Monnette 52. 500 acre tract, Monnette 52; Tinton: Nov. 29, 1685 Resurvey Map; Morris: Nov. 21, 1685 Resurvey.
12. Tinton: Sept. 5, 1676 Acknowledgment; Morris: Feb. 28, 1679 Bill of Sale; Tinton: Draft of Samuel Leonard Property; Miller 65; Tinton: Jan. 30, 1683 Bill of Sale.
13. Morris: Oct. 20, 1676 Carteret Grant.
14. Miller 9.
15. Tinton: Ledger. The first ledger plainly shows Tinton Iron Works, not Tintern Iron Works as claimed by some.
16. Miller 9.
17. Scot 128, 129; Whitehead 402.
18. Cadbury Catalog: 150; Besse 2:315; Flushing 1.
19. Tinton: Ledger.
20. Oldmixon. Winthrop Furnace and Saugus Iron Works in Massachusetts had long since closed. The New Haven Works in Connecticut had closed by 1679 or 80. The Works in the Taunton, Massachusetts, area was still in operation but the output seems to have been small. There is no record of any iron mines in Pennsylvania in the 17th century, although William Penn mentions the existence of iron ore. It seems fair to assume that, during the last quarter of the 17th Century, The Tinton Iron Works, operated by Colonel Lewis Morris, was one of the industrial mainstays of the colonial economy.
21. Tinton: "Draught of Land bought of Samuel Leonard;" Morris: "Lanskip of The Manour of Tinton."

13

Andros-Carteret Arbitrator

Upon the return to America of Governor Edmund Andros of New York and Governor Philip Carteret of New Jersey in October 1674, after the Dutch occupation, Andros, almost immediately, tried to exert influence over Carteret's government in New Jersey. His action was based on the previously noted March 1664 grant of Charles II to his brother, James, Duke of York, for all the land from the Connecticut River to Delaware Bay, including offshore islands, plus Maine east of the Kennebec River, which area included New Jersey. Thus, Andros, regarded Carteret, not as a true governor, but a deputy governor for New Jersey, under Andros. Carteret, however, claimed his right to govern New Jersey independently, based on a June 1664 lease of New Jersey only, from the same James, Duke of York, to Lord John Berkeley and Sir George Carteret.

As governor of New York, Andros was able to impose a customs duty at New York, as previous New York governors had done. But his customs duty of 10% did not bring in expected returns because 10% was too high, which caused great quantities of goods to be smuggled into New England and New Jersey, then brought into New York.[1] In this way, goods arrived in New York duty free—for there was no duty on inter-trade between the settlements of New England, New Jersey and New York.

Colonel Morris and other New York merchants, who were paying the 10% duty, complained of this injustice, so Andros banned this type of relay shipment via New England and New Jersey. He also lowered the customs duty to 5% to encourage merchants to increase their imports, and to make it less attractive for others to smuggle.[2]

These efforts did not appreciably increase shipping nor did they stop some merchants from smuggling. In fact, the Jerseyites complained that they should be paying no customs because they considered themselves not to be under the jurisdiction of Andros.

Finally, Andros was determined to bring the Carteret government under his complete authority. Lewis Morris was to become a direct participant in this controversy.

The matter came to an explosive stage in a routine way, which hit at the very core of the matter.[3] In a letter to Carteret, March 8, 1680, Governor Andros declared his intention to erect a beacon on Sandy Hook in New Jersey, and he agreed to compensate Richard Hartshorne for the use of his land.[4] This was a round-about way of admitting Hartshorne's ownership of the land through the proprietorship of Berkeley and Carteret, (the right to the soil) but denying Governor Carteret's authority to say whether Governor Andros could or could not appropriate the land for government use, (the right to govern).

Less than two weeks after Andros made his demand, Governor Carteret answered that he would try to prevent the construction of the beacon and fort until, "I shall know the Proprietors Pleasure...."[5] Thus, he stood his ground on the right to govern New Jersey through the proprietors.

Two days after dispatching his reply to Andros, Carteret, in anticipation of trouble, vacated the governorship of New Jersey and appointed Captain John Berry acting governor and Captain William Sandford acting deputy governor, in order "to put myself and Country in a Posture of Defense."[6]

All major parties to the dispute were friends of Colonel Lewis Morris. They were Andros, Carteret, Berry and Sandford. Even Hartshorne, who served as the provocation, was a friend and business associate in the Tinton Iron Works.

It was at this stage that Andros decided, possibly at Morris' suggestion, that an attempt be made to settle the matter amicably. There had been rumors circulated in Jersey that Andros was going to use force to obtain his way. Thus, Morris found himself cast in the role of mediator, upon Andros' consent to go to Jersey to talk to Carteret.

When Andros first had come to America, he and Carteret had been reasonably good friends. Carteret frequently had come to New York to attend church, and then visited with Andros at the Fort.

In the interest of conciliation, "It was resolved in Councill [the New

York Council] that the Go: [Governor Andros] goe in person tomar-row in his Sloope towards [Elizabeth Town] New Jersey to be there the next day being the 7th [of April 1680] the time appointed for the De: [Assembly of Deputies] to meete and that he goe in a friendly way with his owne Retinue and some Volunteers to attend him, without other armes than their swords."[7]

Lewis Morris headed the list of "Volunteers" that included govern-ment officials such as James Graham, Attorney General of the province, and Matthias Nicoll, secretary of the province.[8]

There were two boats in the party, the Governor's yacht and the yacht of Colonel Morris. The two vessels set sail about two in the after-noon, on the day following the resolution. After going aground once, they anchored that evening off Staten Island, not far from Elizabeth Town.

As the result of delays, it was decided to send word ahead that same evening to assure Governor Carteret that they were coming in peace. Colonel Morris' craft was dispatched on this mission, with one C. Collyer bearing the message. Colonel Morris and the Governor remained on Andros' yacht.

When Collyer arrived at Elizabeth Town he found it bristling with arms. As he pulled up to the dock, Collyer was met by Captain Sandford, "with his sword drawne." Sandford demanded to know whether they were coming in peace, to which Collyer answered that they were. Collyer was thereupon allowed to tie up and stay the night.

There were conferences that night, and the next morning, after which Collyer returned to Governor Andros and his party. One of the requests made by Carteret, perhaps fearing a coup d'etat, was that a list be submitted of those coming ashore. The next morning at about six, Collyer again left for Elizabeth Town with the list. On reading it, Carteret sent back word that they could proceed.

The way now being clear—Governor Andros, Colonel Morris, and party proceeded to Elizabeth Town in the Governor's and Morris' yachts. Upon landing, the party walked toward Carteret's house on the hill. As the party approached the house, they were met by a company of soldiers. Andros did not stop but kept right on walking and the soldiers parted ranks, allowing Andros and his party to pass. Soon they saw Carteret and a group of officials coming down the hill to greet them. Carteret invited them into the stockade surrounding his house and, as the party passed through the gates, a volley salute was fired.

Friendly greetings were exchanged after which the delegations put their attention to business. First, Andros insisted on reading the King's Charter and the surrender document from the Dutch. While this was going on in grand oratorical display, the citizenry crowded around hoping to hear what was being said, but Captain Sandford brusquely herded all those not officially there, out of the stockade.

Andros then demanded that his charter be read outside, which was done. When this was completed, Carteret suggested that Andros, Morris and the party come into Carteret's house, where they could talk and discuss the matter quietly.

When they arrived inside, Captain John Berry became the principal spokesman for Carteret. He produced and read documents of the proprietors' authorization. There were discussions and arguments back and forth for some time, all revolving around whether the Duke's patent (Andros' authority) had greater weight than the Duke's lease (Carteret's authority). Berry's final statement was that an appeal should be made to England to resolve the whole matter of the right to govern New Jersey.

By this time it was late in the day, and with nothing settled, Governor Andros, Colonel Morris and the New York party walked down to the dock, accompanied by Carteret and Berry. They boarded their yachts and, having a good wind, they reached New York that night. Morris had failed in his effort to arbitrate the matter to a compromise solution. Now, feelings were more bitter than ever.

Three weeks after the mediation efforts, a party of soldiers, sent by Andros, came ashore in Elizabeth Town at night, and captured Carteret while he slept. Andros is said to have bribed one of the domestics of the Carteret household into giving him information as to when and how to make the capture. Knowing from this inside source that Carteret had no soldiers guarding him at night, Andros had equipped some yachts and a ketch with heavily armed soldiers and gave them instructions to capture Carteret, and bring him back to New York.

The intruders landed quietly and entered the Carteret house at midnight, "seized him naked, dragged him through the window, struck and kicked him terribly, and even injured him internally. They threw him, all naked as he was, into a canoe, without any cap or hat on his head, and carried him in that condition to New York, and then conducted him to the fort and put him immediately in prison."[9]

Carteret's account of his own capture stated that Andros: "sent a party of soldiers to fetch me away dead or alive, so that in the dead time of night broke open my doors and most barbarously and inhumanly and violently halled me out of my bed, that I have not words enough sufficiently to express the cruelty of it; and indeed I am so disabled by the bruises and hurts I then received, that I fear I shall hardly be a perfect man again."[10]

Carteret was kept in prison three days short of a month, when a special Court of Assizes was convened to try him. Andros had a seat erected in the courtroom, high above all the others, and he entered the courtroom at each session to the blare of trumpets. Governor Carteret was treated as an ordinary criminal.

The evidence was heard and exhibits examined. It was a jury trial and Andros acted, throughout, as though he were the prosecuting attorney. The final blows were struck when Andros declared that he had never regarded Carteret as governor of New Jersey, whereupon Carteret drew from his pocket several letters from Andros, all addressed to "The Governor of New Jersey." Andros replied that because he called him "Governor" did not make it so. Whereupon Carteret produced a letter from the King, also addressing him as "Governor of New Jersey."

The jury retired and soon brought in a verdict of "not guilty." Andros tried to get the jury to reconsider by sending them out again, and then again. When this failed, Andros agreed to drop the charges if Carteret agreed to refrain from exercising his authority in New Jersey until the matter could be settled by the authorities in England.

The British authorities withheld their decision from Carteret for almost a year. In the end, they reached a conclusion in his favor. Carteret had won a victory and he resumed exercising his authority in New Jersey.

A man with the determination of Andros was not one to give up so easily on measures to increase revenue. Andros controlled the North, or Hudson River, and still was able to impose customs duties there.

In order to increase revenues, Andros prohibited the distilling of spiritous liquors in the province of New York.[11] This immediately resulted in the importation of huge quantities of taxable liquor from abroad. Rum sales were greatly increased by this regulation. The advantage to Colonel Morris and other importers of rum was further enhanced by a new rate of import tax imposed by Andros, which favored West Indian rum over all other liquors.[12]

With this favorable duty, and consequent lower selling price, the demand for rum increased many fold. It soon became in short supply. Prices of rum skyrocketed and the Barbados merchants, of which Colonel Morris was among the most important, were reaping huge returns.

Enemies of Andros accused him of being implicated. In fact, it was openly charged that he was in outright partnership with certain New York merchants, and that he was sharing in their huge profits.[13]

As a result of these and other serious charges of dishonesty, Andros was summoned to England. He embarked January 7, 1682. When brought to account, he was able to refute the charges of dishonesty, and later he was made "Gentleman of the Privy Council" by Charles II.

Carteret was not as fortunate. He was forced to resign as Governor because his proprietors had sold their interest in New Jersey, and Carteret died in December 1682, less than two months after his resignation. Some say he died from the injuries inflicted at the time of his abduction by Andros' men.

An interesting sidelight to this whole affair is the fact that much of what is known today of this Andros-Carteret encounter was found in the diary of two Labadist missionaries who were in New York in 1679 and 1680.[14] Whether their report partially reflected Morris' version of this conflict, is not known. But it should be noted that they met and traveled by ferry, from Morrisania to Harlem, with the Colonel and Walter Webley, Jr., while the Andros-Carteret matter was fresh in everyone's mind.

1. Danckaerts 353.
2. 1 NJA 1:289–291.
3. L and S 673 et seq.
4. 1 NJA 1:292.
5. Ibid: 294.
6. Ibid: 295.
7. Ibid: 299.
8. Ibid: 299 et seq.
9. Danckaerts 346 et seq.
10. Hatfield 192.
11. Danckaerts 354.
12. Liquor Laws 109.
13. Danckaerts 354; Whitmore 20,21; NYD 2:284, 302–308.
14. Danckaerts 346–352.

14

Early
Quaker

George Fox founded the Quaker religion in 1650 or 1652, in England. Within four years from that founding, Lewis Morris, while still in Barbados, became interested in the movement. This was apparent not long after Morris was involved with Venables and Penn over joining the expedition to Hispaniola and Jamaica, and not long after he was elevated to the Governing Council of Barbados, in March 1656.

A letter to Margaret Fell, later to become the wife of George Fox, is indicative of Lewis Morris' early interest in the movement. The letter was dated "19 of 10th month [December] 1656," written from Barbados and signed Henry Fell, a Quaker missionary there. The two Fells were apparently not closely, if at all related.

The letter stated: "The Governor [Searle] here is pretty moderate and some of the great ones, whereby persecution is something restrained Here is one call Collo. Morris in whom [is] some desires and love unto the Truth. He had a desire to see me, so I was free to go to his house and he was very loving to me. But by the way I was passing thither I was much abused and beaten, it being not far from him. I was free to acquaint him with the manner of it and he was much troubled at it. So he told me he would have the men before the Governor and said that the Governor he was sure would punish them and would not suffer any to abuse me if he knew of it. I hear since that they are bound over to their [court of] sessions as they call them."[1]

By 1656, the year of the Fell letter, converts were coming to Quakerism in great numbers, not only in Britain but also in the West Indies, particularly in Barbados. "In Barbados the Society grew rapidly, increasing by settlers from England and by convincements, until it became an influential body of friends. These included Thomas

Rous, formerly a Lieutenant Colonel, whose son John traveled in the ministry and later married Margaret, daughter of [Thomas and] Margaret Fell; [and] Lewis Morris formerly a Colonel and member of the Council.''[2] The word "formerly," used with respect to the military commissions held by Rous and Morris, suggests that both had given up the military because of their religion.

By 1666 Lewis Morris, now a leader in the movement, was referred to as "of good interest and conduct and an honest man though a Quaker.''[3] In 1668, he was referred to by Governor William Lord Willoughby of Barbados as one of the commissioners of that island but a "severe Quaker.''[4]

Over the years there were many exchanges of correspondence between George Fox and Lewis Morris, the following being one of the more important, not for content but for results.[5] In 1669, George Fox wrote to Morris about helping a young man by the name of William Fortiscue, who was fatherless. The letter was one of three brought to light many years later by the anti-Quakers to show, as they believed, that Fox was not capable of writing the epistles and additional works attributed to him. The other two letters were doctrinal in content.

One Daniel Leeds of Burlington, New Jersey, obtained these three letters written by Fox to Lewis Morris. They indicated that Fox was not a good speller, and Leeds, with possibly others encouraging him, reasoned that because Fox's epistles and writings did not contain numerous misspelled words, which the letters did, that the epistles attributed to him could not have been written by Fox. Daniel Leeds published his work in New York and he called it *The Mystery of Fox-Craft*.[6] The publication was widely used in America against the Quakers, mainly by the Anglicans under George Keith, who had formerly been a Quaker preacher, Surveyor General of East Jersey, and an employee of Colonel Lewis Morris.[7]

In 1671, George Fox decided on a trip to North America, where the Quaker movement had achieved considerable success. Enroute, Fox stopped at Barbados to visit with, and inspire, the Quakers there. He stayed three months in Barbados but was ill most of the time. His illness has since been diagnosed as rheumatic fever.[8] While in Barbados, Fox could neither walk nor ride most of the time, and the work of holding meetings had to be left to his associates. Fox resided with Thomas

Rous, but was anxious to visit Lewis Morris, where "his company is desired."[9]

Finally, Fox felt well enough to visit the Governor at Bridge Town, then proceeded to Lewis Morris'.[10] In a letter from John Stubbs, one of Fox's seven traveling companions, to Margaret Fox, Stubbs stated: "Lewis Morris, Thomas Rous, and I think his two sons and John Hull [another of Fox's traveling companions] with other friends, went along [to the Governor's] with thy husband and there they continued most part of the day and dined there also. . . .

"Then after the meeting he [Fox] passed to Lewis Morris' house that night which was about nine or ten miles distant partly performing his journey along the sea coast in a boat ['the rest by horseback', says Fox in his journal]; and there he continued about a week. There is the finest air in the island about Lewis' plantation."[11]

Upon his return to health, Fox and his party got under way to Jamaica, where they remained seven weeks. From there, they proceeded to Maryland. Following a sojourn in Maryland, they started north, crossing the Delaware River at New Castle, Delaware. From there, they proceeded overland, via what was later to be known as the Burlington Path, to Middletown, New Jersey, then to New England and back to New Jersey via Middletown and Shrewsbury.

There is evidence suggesting that Lewis Morris may have accompanied George Fox to America, or at least was at New Castle in the spring of 1672, when Fox arrived there. Fox crossed the Delaware River into New Jersey from New Castle in March, 1672. On July 26, 1672, four months after the crossing, Lewis Morris and his brother Richard were granted 1,000 acres in New Jersey "over against New Castle" at what was probably the very place of crossing.[12]

The period between the crossing and the Morris grant provided just enough lapsed time for Lewis Morris to proceed to Elizabeth Town to make his request for land before his old friends and associates, Captain John Berry, Captain William Sandford and James Bollen. Governor Carteret had left for England a month before and John Berry was acting governor at the time.

The remarkable thing about the New Jersey grant, as noted before, is that it was made about three years prior to any other recorded English grant in West New Jersey. Describing West Jersey in 1672,

Fox wrote in his journal as he crossed the Delaware, "Then we had that wilderness to pass through since called West Jersey, not then inhabited by the English...."

Fox, on the first leg of his return home to England, retraced his steps through the heart of New Jersey over the so-called Burlington Path, then to Virginia. Fox stayed a few days in Virginia, then left for England, arriving at Bristol, June 20, 1673, a month before the Dutch retook New York. It had been a long and difficult pilgrimage.

In Barbados, the situation improved but little for the Quakers after Fox left. The anti-Quakers continued to harass and abuse them. They also taxed and fined them heavily for not contributing to the army, either physically or financially, and for not paying for the support of the established church of England.

For example, Lewis Morris, although residing much of the time in New York, was fined 16,193 pounds of sugar in Barbados over a four-year period from 1674–78 for "not sending horses and men to the militia and paying church dues." His name headed at least two petitions in Barbados sent to Governor Atkins, in 1677 and 1678, protesting discriminatory abuses against the Quakers.[13]

These surely were some of the reasons, in addition to economic pressures, why Lewis Morris decided, about 1678 or 79, to dispose of all of his interests in Barbados. New York, at that time, was fairly tolerant as far as religious freedom was concerned. New Jersey was extremely favorable in this regard.

1. Swarthmore Mss. 1:67.
2. JFHS: Supplement Tortola; Besse 2:315.
3. CO Col. Papers Vol. XX #145; CSPC 1661–1668:413.
4. CO Col. Papers Vol. XXII #60; CSPC 1661–1668:556.
5. Cadbury Catalog: 134; Swarthmore Mss. iii:108.
6. Leeds; Bugg.
7. Tinton: Ledger.
8. Baker 136.
9. Nickalls: 597.
10. Shilstone-Bajan: Sept. 1960:19.
11. Nickalls: 600.
12. Salem Deed Book B: 10, 86, 113; 1 NJA 21:565, etc. A possible outgrowth of the grant to Colonel Morris in 1672 of 1,000 acres in the Salem Cove–Finns Point area of New Jersey "over against New Castle" may have been the Quaker purchase of Lord John Berkeley's one half interest in New Jersey in 1674 and the settlement at Salem in 1675; and at Burlington in 1677.
13. Besse 2:313–315; NYD 2:619; Fox 430.

15

American
Statesman

On February 1, 1682, William Penn and eleven associates, later enlarged to 24, bought one half of New Jersey from Sir George Carteret's widow for £3,400, the land to become known as East New Jersey.[1]

William Penn and another group of Quaker associates, as trustees for Edward Billing, previously had acquired, in 1674, Lord John Berkeley's one half interest in New Jersey, the land to become known as West New Jersey.[2] These two halves earlier had been held jointly by Berkeley and Carteret. By agreement, the line between the divided New Jersey was to run northwest to southeast from the northern most branch of the Delaware at 41° and 40' north latitude to Little Egg Harbor on the eastern coast of New Jersey.

Thomas Rudyard, a British Quaker was chosen to be resident head of the East Jersey government, and Lewis Morris was chosen to be the chief of Rudyard's governing council.[3]

As soon as possible, Colonel Morris built a home in East Jersey, at Shrewsbury, on the west edge of Shrewsbury village, about a mile from his Tinton Iron Works.[4] Within a short time after building a residence, the Colonel was elected deputy to the East New Jersey Legislature from Shrewsbury, but he declined that elective office upon taking his place as a member of the Governing Council.[5]

On February 12, 1683, Colonel Lewis Morris took his seat at Elizabeth Town as head of Governor Rudyard's East New Jersey Council.[6] Although he was a newcomer to government in New Jersey, he was no newcomer to high level government. He had started public service over a quarter of a century earlier when, in 1656, he was elected to the legislative assembly in Barbados and the next year was chosen, by the governor there, to serve on his council. For many years following, Lewis Morris served simultaneously on the Governing Council of Barbados and as a member of its highest court.[7] He was also one of the Home Government Commissioners for the island.[8]

It is significant that the Colonel's executive, judicial and legislative experience had been acquired in Barbados where representative government and virtual self government had flourished for many years. Lewis Morris was a reservoir of experience as he helped Thomas Rudyard set up a democracy in East New Jersey, which type government had not existed under the Philip Carteret regime, except in a limited sense during its first few months.

In a letter to William Penn on February 13, 1682, the day after the first meeting of Rudyard's council, Rudyard wrote to Penn telling him of his selection of Lewis Morris and a few other men of "reputation" to serve on his council.[9] In the same letter he told of his troubles with Samuel Groome, one of the proprietors, who was also surveyor general for East New Jersey. Rudyard described Groome as having "grown into an angry pettish humor." This break with Groome was basically because Rudyard would not permit Groome to dictate who would serve on Rudyard's governing council.

In an attempt to resolve the quarrel, Lewis Morris talked to Groome, but Groome merely said he resented Rudyard, yet would give no reasons. Charges flew back and forth between Rudyard and Groome, with Morris acting as a referee. Rudyard charged Groome with trying to get people on the council who would assist Groome "in private trade and commerce." Groome charged Rudyard with favoritism and improper procedure in hearing cases, plus a charge bordering on dishonesty in Rudyard's handling of accounts.

The quarrel took on much more significance when Lewis Morris reported to Rudyard that Richard Hartshorne, Morris' neighbor, business associate and fellow Quaker, had been persuaded by Groome to head a revolt of patentees. The object was to re-establish their Nicolls land patents, which they had earlier agreed to relinquish. In an effort to put down this revolt, Lewis Morris suggested that he take Rudyard, in his personal sloop, from Elizabeth Town to the Sandy Hook area, where Hartshorne resided, so that Rudyard and Morris could "quench ye flame."[10]

When Morris and Rudyard could not prevent Groome from his dis-

PLATE 7

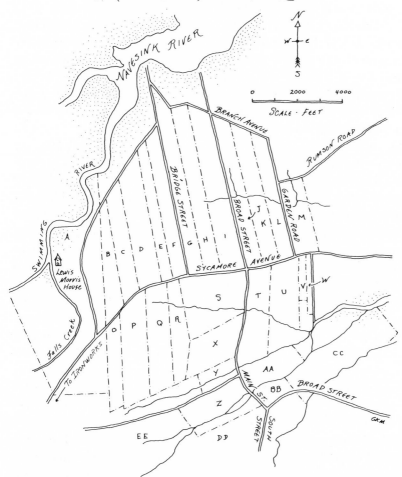

SHREWSBURY TOWN LOTS

A. Col. Lewis Morris, 500 acres, B. Samuel Wolcott, C. Stephen West, D. Peter Tilton, E. John Slocum, F. Peter Parker, G. Hannah Jay (alias Cook), H. Remembrance Lippincott, I.Judah Allen, J. John Lippincott, K. Francis Borden, L. Gideon Freeborne, M. Joseph Parker, O. Robert West, P. Edmund Lafetra, Q. John Haven, R. Judah Allen, S. William West (son of Mrs. N. Browne, widow of Christopher West), T. Nicholas Browne, U. John Worthley, V. Ephraim Allen, W. Joseph Parker, X. John Champnes, Y. Nicholas Browne, Z. Eliakim Wardell, AA. Eliakim Wardell, BB. Eliakim Wardell, CC. Jacob Coale, DD. Jedediah Allen, EE. Hannah Jay (alias Cook).

ruptive activity, Rudyard wrote Penn asking him to come to New Jersey, if possible, and to do so when the Assembly was to meet, to see if he could resolve the quarrel. Although Penn was a very small shareholder in East New Jersey, he, as indicated by his letters preserved in the Friends Library, London, was directing the overall policy of East New Jersey's government, as he was doing in West New Jersey and in Pennsylvania.[11]

But all was not bickering in the Rudyard-Morris regime. One of the first acts passed under their government was to divide East New Jersey into four counties—Bergen, Essex, Middlesex and Monmouth—and to direct the election of deputies from each county. Representatives from each would constitute the legislative assembly.[12]

Robert Hunter Morris, great nephew of Colonel Morris, in a letter eighty years later, wrote that he had "always understood" that the Colonel asked that Monmouth County be so named after Monmouthshire, England, where the Colonel is said to have been born.[13] The family legend may be true, but there is neither a documented record of the Colonel's request nor a record of his birth there.

Among the acts that were passed by the Rudyard-Morris government, was one to reorganize the structure of the court system. Pursuant to this act, Colonel Lewis Morris was chosen chief of the Court of Sessions, which was to meet twice a year in each of the four counties.[14]

Each county was, for the first time, to have a high sheriff. All matters out of the county courts (Court of Sessions) were to go through him. Lewis Morris, son of Thomas, became the first high sheriff of Monmouth County.[15]

Another advanced step was that, in the court of small causes held before local magistrates, either party could demand a trial by jury, no matter how insignificant the amount or conditions involved.

Colonel Lewis Morris was also selected to be presiding officer of the Court of Common Right, a new court to take the place of the Court of Assizes.[16] It was to be the supreme court of East New Jersey. By the Colonel's appointment to this supreme body, he became the highest judicial officer in East New Jersey, as well as the chief administrative officer, the Governor excepted.

Many additional truly democratic acts were passed during the Rudyard-Morris tenure, some of them having been outlined in the

Concessions and Agreements brought over by Carteret but not put into effect—and some of them entirely new, many having a Barbadian flavor. For example, no freeman was to be imprisoned except after a fair trial and pursuant to judgment by his peers. Laws controlling imprisonment for debt were enacted requiring, in some cases, the plaintiff to post a bond prior to the granting of a warrant for arrest. Trading in negro slaves was prohibited, and dealing with the Indians was regulated.

During the second session of the Rudyard council, William Penn was in attendance, sitting as one of the proprietors. He attended the council five days consecutively.[17] It was a distinguished occasion for Lewis Morris to have this great Quaker leader and "honored friend" at his side. In attendance, also, was Samuel Groome, who shortly thereafter was to cause the downfall of the Rudyard government.

The events leading to this were as follows: The planned procedure for allocating land called for the division of all large tracts into seven parts. One of these parts was to be set aside for the proprietors. Groome refused to survey any land pursuant to warrants issued by Governor Rudyard unless provision was made for the proprietor's one seventh to be set forth in the warrant for survey itself. Rudyard and Morris maintained that it was not necessary to authorize, specifically, the reservation of the one seventh in each warrant but that it could be handled later and separately.[18] The proprietors sided with Groome, and after serving just one year as governor, Rudyard was replaced by Gawen Lawrie.

Lawrie, a London merchant and staunch Quaker, already was deeply involved in the affairs of West Jersey as one of the trustees for Edward Billing. Lawrie retained Colonel Lewis Morris as a member of his East Jersey council and on the bench of the Court of Common Right, the supreme court.[19]

While Morris was a member of the East New Jersey supreme court and council, he also sat, from 1683–1686, on the New York Governing Council under Governor Thomas Dongan.[20] Dongan had arrived in New York August 25, 1683, replacing Andros, who returned to England.

Dongan's new New York council, with the Colonel sitting as a member, immediately proceeded with the establishment of a democratic form of government, by electing a General Assembly. This was the first elected assembly of the province of New York and it met within the walls of Fort James. The assembly passed fifteen acts, the most outstanding of which was "The Charter of Libertyes and Priviledges. . . ." This charter was a landmark in American legislative action. The charter was vetoed by the King, yet it pointed the way to future democratic advances.

The Dongan government soon set up a new court system in 1683, as had been done in East New Jersey, and made further improvements in the system the next year. In this, Colonel Morris was actively involved.

Colonel Lewis Morris' position of simultaneously serving as a member of the governing council of New York and East New Jersey, as well as on the highest court of East New Jersey, was unusual, if not precarious. Governor Dongan was interested, as Andros had been, in taking over the governments of East and West New Jersey, so that he could control smuggling and collect more taxes.

In August, 1684, James, Duke of York, wrote to Dongan stating: "if you find that ye inhabitants of New Jersey have any other way of trading with the Indians than by the Province of New Yorke, that you will endeavor to prevent it. . . my desire being to preserve the Indian trade as entire as I can for the benefit of the inhabitants and traders of New York preferably to all others."[21]

This was unmistakable authorization for Dongan to proceed in any way he thought best to protect the trade of the New York merchants, of which Lewis Morris was still one of the most important.

By April 1685, Governor Dongan of New York had installed a tax collector in East New Jersey. But the Jerseyites, in defiance, acquitted anyone who was arrested and tried for bringing goods into New Jersey without paying a tax.

Despite this economic war, Morris retained his seat on the East New Jersey Council even after the council noted that "Coll Morris being mostly absent and Liveing in the Province of New Yorke. . .It was necessary to appoint others as addicon to the former Councill. . . ." Further, the Colonel was appointed to the Court of Common Right in East New Jersey as late as May 27, 1685.[22]

During his many-faceted governmental tenure in both New York and New Jersey, the Colonel was again cast in the role of mediator. This time it was between Governors Lawrie of East New Jersey and

Dongan of New York with respect to the boundary line between New York and New Jersey. The location of this line was important also in determining the line separating East and West New Jersey.

Lewis Morris was an expert on matters of this nature, having been a navigator and surveyor most of his adult life. He owned a very accurate surveying instrument, a "sextile" (as close as can be determined a large land sextant), which he had earlier loaned to William Penn and Lord Baltimore to help them settle their boundary line controversy between Maryland and Pennsylvania.[23]

Sometime prior to April 1684, Governors Dongan and Lawrie met and agreed to abide by the boundary set forth in the Berkeley-Carteret Grant.[24] But it was not until two years later, in 1686, that the actual boundary was examined by a board of three surveyors representing the two Jerseys and New York. At these field meetings, a dispute arose among the three surveyors over the location of the line, and the matter was not settled, although many sights were taken.

That same year the two Governors, Dongan and Lawrie, together with their councils, met on the west side of the Hudson River to view the problem, first hand. Colonel Morris was serving on both councils at the time. It is very probable that he, personally, took observations with his sextile at this high level field-surveying party. The Colonel's sextile was the "only fixt instrument yt. could be heard of" and it had a "six or seven foot radius."[25] Finally, a beech tree lying beside a small run was marked with a pen knife and the meeting adjourned.

An important sidelight to this whole affair lies in the fact that his ward Lewis Morris, son of Richard, age fifteen at the time, was at this governor's field conference.[26] Fifty years later young Lewis Morris, then governor of New Jersey, made a signed statement relative to the East-West Jersey line, over which, at that late date, controversy still existed. In his testimony, Governor Lewis Morris told about the locating of a point on the Hudson and the marking of a tree by the joint councils. Then, he said that he, personally, returned there five years later and remarked the same tree.

In the next few years, young Lewis would become so accomplished in the profession of law under the tutelage of his uncle and guardian, the Colonel, that, at age twenty, he would be a judge of the Court of Sessions in East New Jersey, and at twenty-one, on the Governing

Council of East New Jersey.[27] Still in his twenties, he would become president of the Governing Council of East New Jersey.

When only thirty-one, in 1702, young Lewis Morris made a trip abroad and appeared before Queen Anne urging Her Majesty to take over both Jerseys from the quarreling proprietary governments, which she did. Shortly thereafter, he was named Governor of a combined East and West New Jersey, but the order was withdrawn in favor of Viscount Edward Cornbury, the Queen's cousin, so that he could govern both New York and the two New Jersies.

By 1710, Lewis Morris, age 38, became the head of Governor Robert Hunter's New York governing council. The next year he was appointed to the supreme court of New York and then elevated to chief justice—serving as chief justice of New York for the next twenty years.

In 1738, Lewis Morris, age 66, became the first royal Governor of New Jersey, which was now being separated as an independent province. Lewis Morris served as governor of New Jersey until his death in 1746, a term of eight years.

An illustration of Colonel Lewis Morris' influence on colonial affairs through his nephew and ward Lewis, long after the Colonel's departure from the scene, is found in the John Peter Zenger case of 1733, which established the doctrine of "freedom of the press" in America.

The matter involved young Lewis Morris, when he was Chief Justice of New York, in a conflict between Rip Van Dam, president of the governing council of New York, and Governor Cosby. It concerned Van Dam's pay as acting governor of New York during the period between the death of Governor Montgomery and the start of Governor Cosby's term.

In support of Van Dam's effort to keep what he had already been paid, Chief Justice Lewis Morris prepared a long argument, and gave it wide verbal publicity. Governor Cosby was very displeased and demanded a copy of Morris' argument. Morris thereupon had his argument printed by John Peter Zenger, a New York printer and publisher, and sent a copy to the Governor. As a result, Zenger was arrested and charged with criminal libel against the province, but he was acquitted.

Rather than going deeply into the matter of "freedom of the press," it seems sufficient here to quote from a 20th century eminent jurist's review of the case, which brought out the fact that Chief Justice Morris' principal argument in support of Van Dam's claim was based on the history, structure and intentions of the acts setting up the New York court system. The review stated further: "It is noteworthy that the language of the New York Acts and ordinances cited by Chief Justice Morris. . . is substantially duplicated in the New Jersey charters and ordinances."[28]

It is even more "noteworthy" when it is realized that it was Colonel Lewis Morris who was one of the principal architects of both the New York and New Jersey "charters and ordinances" and that it was the Colonel's star pupil who, 50 years later, was expounding arguments on the history, structure and intentions of the "charters and ordinances."

To illustrate how deep was the penetration of the Morris clan into New York and New Jersey affairs during the first half of the 18th century, we recite a few examples. To keep straight the several Lewis Morrises to be mentioned, we will designate the Colonel's ward, Lewis Morris, son of Richard, "Lewis I," etc.

When Lewis I vacated his position on the New York Governing Council to go to the supreme court, his son Lewis II was appointed to the New York council.[29] When Lewis I became governor of New Jersey, another son, Robert Hunter Morris, went on his father's governing council, then became Chief Justice of the New Jersey Supreme Court.[30] Robert Hunter Morris later became governor of Pennsylvania. Further, Robert Hunter Morris' son, Robert, became the first Chief Justice of New Jersey, after the Revolution.[31]

In-laws also came in for their share of public service. Lewis I's father-in-law, James Graham, became Attorney General of New York, New Jersey and Connecticut.[32] Lewis I's brother-in-law, Augustus Graham, became surveyor general of New York.[33]

When Lewis I became governor of New Jersey, in addition to appointing his son Robert Hunter Morris to his council, he also appointed to his council, son-in-law Edward Antill II [34] as well as the father-in-law of his daughter Isabella, Richard Ashfield, Sr.[35] Isabella's son, Lewis Morris Ashfield, later was to serve on the same council.[36] Another son-in-law of Lewis Morris I, Michael Kearny, became secretary of the province and treasurer of the East Division of

New Jersey.[37] With these numerous appointments, there were loud cries of nepotism throughout New Jersey.

To add a final glowing touch to 18th century Morris statesmanship, Lewis Morris II had three sons who continued the family tradition of law and public service. Son Richard Morris became chief justice of New York and was one of the framers of the New York State Constitution.[38] Son Lewis Morris III was a signer of the Declaration of Independence, from New York.[39] Son Gouverneur Morris became United States Senator from New York, minister to France after the Revolution, and a writer of the final draft of the Constitution of the United States.[40]

---

1. Analytical Index Feb. 1, 1682; 1 NJA 1:366.
2. 1 NJA 1:324.
3. 1 NJA 13:3.
4. Tinton: Ledger; Monnette 52.
5. 1 NJA 13:7.
6. Ibid: 3.
7. Journal Aug. 1943:176; Acts: 22, Act of Jan. 15, 1655.
8. CO Col Papers Vol. XXII #60; CSPC 1661–1668:556.
9. Penn Papers No. 7.
10. Ibid: 7, 8, 11, 12.
11. Ibid.
12. Whitehead 128 et seq.; Leaming and Spicer.
13. Morris RHM 1763 Corres.
14. 1 NJA 13:40, 41; Applegate 5.
15. 1 NJA 13:24.
16. Ibid: 99.
17. Ibid: 6.
18. Ibid: 101.
19. Ibid: 120, 121; Whitehead 132 note 3.
20. Stillwell 4:5; Akerly.
21. 1 NJA 1:475, 491, 524; Whitehead 143, 144.
22. 1 NJA 13:120, 142; Whitehead 132 note.
23. Pa. Mag. 6:416, 430; Hall 427.
24. 1 PNJHS 8:160 et seq.; 1 NJA 1:517, 518; 1 NJA 2:22–24; Monnette 548; Miller 4.
25. Pa. Mag. 6:416–430; CSPC 1681–1685:351.
26. 1 NJA 1:521.
27. Kemmerer; Papers; 1 NJA 13:192; Stillwell 4:25.
28. PNJHS Apr. 1937:87 et seq.
29. Stillwell 4:36.
30. Kemmerer 359, 360; Stillwell 4:36.
31. McCormick 116 note 42.
32. Analytical Index 14.
33. Monnette 1122.
34. Papers 122; Kemmerer 359; Stillwell 4:35, 38.
35. Papers 122; Kemmerer 195, 196.

36. Kemmerer 359; Stillwell 4:38.
37. Kemmerer 363; Stillwell 3:389.
38. Stillwell 4:43.
39. Ibid. Robert Morris, another signer, was not related.
40. Ibid; Britannica; Diary.

16

Life
At
Morrisania

Gouverneur Morris, the fourth generation of Morrises to occupy the ancestral home of Morrisania, entered in his diary on January 5, 1788, "Today...I...go after dinner to my house at Morrisania, where I arrive at dusk, after an absence of about 10 years."[1] This brief diary entry gives little hint to the sad story of Morrisania during the period of the American Revolution.

Briefly, what had happened during that 10 year period was this. Gouverneur had graduated from Kings College in 1768. He was admitted to the bar three years later in 1771, and by 1775, he was elected to the Provincial Congress of New York. At the outbreak of the Revolutionary War, Gouverneur Morris spoke out for independence, as did his older half brother, Lewis Morris III, a member of Congress —to which body Gouverneur would soon be elected.

When the war moved from New England to the New York area, in the late summer of 1776, Gouverneur became worried about the safety of his widowed mother, Sarah Gouverneur Morris who was living at Morrisania. It is not known when Sarah Morris left Morrisania, but by January 19, 1777, a few months after the Battle of Long Island, and after the British occupation of New York, it was reported that "At Morrisania, the family vault was opened, the coffins broken, and the bones scattered abroad."[2] Sarah's departed husband, Lewis Morris II, was in one of those robbed graves on the Morrisania property.

During the remaining years of the Revolution, both Manhattan and Long Islands were occupied by the British, and Morrisania became virtually a no-man's land—lying between British forces on Manhattan and Long Islands and American forces still holding upper Westchester County. The Americans made frequent raids on Morrisania, but for much of the period of the war, Morrisania was occupied by a corps of Loyalist cavalry under the command of Lt. Col. James Delancey. Locally, these men were called "Delancey's cowboys," for their rough riding and equally rough manners.

When the war was over, and Sarah Morris returned to Morrisania, she found that her home and property had been horribly damaged. Son Gouverneur assisted her in making a survey of damages, after which Sarah made an application to the government for reparations, and was granted "8,000 pounds."[3]

After his mother's death in 1786, Gouverneur purchased other inherited interests in the old Morrisania house. He then tore down the war ravaged structure and built a new house on the old foundation. In a letter to a friend, Gouverneur wrote, "No, I have built no castle, but a pretty good house at Morrisania, on the foundation of that in which I was born and in which my parents died."[4]

Thus, the sprawling, frequently added to, 150 year old structure, which was begun by Jonas Bronx in 1639, quietly came to an end. The location of the house had been noted first on a 1639 map, titled DE MANATUS OP DE NOORT RIUIER and described in the text of the map as "43: Begonnen Bou Van Jonas Bronx," translated as "the building in the first stages of progress by Jonas Bronx."[5]

Although these first beginnings probably were quite small, the house did have a superb view, looking almost straight down the East River. It was set back from the water's edge on a rise of about 40 feet, with a small stream, called Mill Brook, running slightly east of the house. In modern terms of reference, the house stood just northwest of the corner of Brown Place and East 132nd Street, in the Borough of Bronx, New York.

Soon after starting to build his house, Jonas Bronx began leasing some of his 500 acres to those who would guarantee to clear and cultivate the land, which was then very wooded. Two of these lessees were "Peter Andriessen and Lourent Dayts."[6] But, when Colonel Lewis Morris purchased the property in 1668, these small operations came to an end. Under the Morris ownership, several out-buildings were soon erected and, over the years, the main house was added to several times, until it measured "one hundred and thirty feet long."[7]

The new out-buildings that were built included a blacksmith shop, barns, granaries, storerooms and quarters for 66 Negroes, namely "22 man negroes, 11 women, 6 boys, 2 garles, 25 children."[8] There also was a house on the property occupied by Mr. Osborne, foreman of the manor. Most of the Negroes worked at husbandry, while a few of them did servant work in the main house. In the main house, lived the Colonel, his second wife, Mary, and his ward, Lewis I, son of the Colonel's deceased brother, Richard.

Young Lewis seems to have begun his education at an early age. It is said that "Hugh Coppathwait, a Quaker zealot was his preceptor."[9] This may have been the Hugh Cowperthwaite (with varied spellings) who with his wife, Grace, lived in Flushing, New York. It is known that an Elizabeth Coperthwait, possibly a sister, kept a school in Flushing from 1675–1681

William Bickley, the Colonel's first servant, and his family lived off the manor property at Devoe's Point, just north of Cromwell Creek, which flowed into the Harlem River opposite about what is now 155th Street, Manhattan. Bickley spent much of his time at Morrisania, and he may have had some quarters in the main house.

The Colonel's nephew, Walter Webley, Jr., son of the Colonel's sister, and his family lived in Harlem, just across the Harlem River Ferry from Morrisania. The ferry, established in 1667, had its Harlem terminus at what is now 125th Street and its Westchester terminus in Bronx Kill near the foot of what is now Brook Avenue.

Webley was an attorney, as was the Colonel and his brother, Richard. It is probable that Webley was trained either by the Colonel or Richard or both. Webley took over much of the Colonel's legal work after the death of Richard, and he appears to have been an almost daily visitor at Morrisania.

At the height of development of Morrisania under Colonel Lewis Morris, the estate contained "one thousand nine hundred and twenty acres." For all of this property, Morris, in 1676, was issued a new patent by his friend, Royal Governor Edmund Andros, for which the Colonel was to pay in taxes the small sum of "five bushels of good winter wheat," annually.[10]

Because the Colonel was a staunch Quaker, it is assumed that there was little frivolous party giving at Morrisania. However, the Colonel did seem to enjoy music, particularly the lute. In the inventory of his goods is listed "39 yards [of] lutestring."[11] No liquors or wines appear in any of the inventories of goods at Morrisania, yet, the Colonel was probably the largest importer of rum in the colonies.

The Colonel's wife, Mary, seems to have dressed in suitable Quaker fashion. In her inventory is recorded "30 yards...of black silk prunella [and] 16 pr. of women's worsted hose."[12]

In his later years, the Colonel became quite active in New York and Flushing Quaker circles, and at one time he allowed Morrisania to be used as a meetinghouse. At the Flushing Meeting, it was recorded and "agreed that whereas the weekly fifth meeting of friends in New York have been late neglected and they desiring ye meeting to take care of ye establishment thereof...that the 1st day meeting shall remain at Robert Storys and ye fifth day meeting at Lewis Morris house until a public meeting house shall be provided."[13]

Not only was the Colonel active in Quaker affairs, he seems to have taken an interest in all religions and all churches. For example, when St. Peter's Church of Westchester had no bell to call the members to worship, the Colonel gave them a bell and had it inscribed on the lip, "Colonel Lewis Morris 1677."[14]

For personal transportation, in addition to numerous carriages and horses, the Colonel maintained good docking facilities near the main house. Frequently, it is recorded that vessels of considerable size docked at Morrisania. For his personal use, he maintained "1 sloop and yall, 1 yall and pinnace."[15] Of course these were in addition to a large fleet of ships the Colonel maintained in New York for the conduct of his vast iron and sugar businesses.

Morrisania was the Colonel's home, and he appears to have taken great pains to maintain privacy and simplicity of living there, despite his considerable wealth and connections. Above all, Morrisania seems not to have been regarded as a money making establishment.

The 2,000 acres of Morrisania could have supported literally hundreds of livestock, yet there were only enough to satisfy the needs of the manor. Livestock at Morrisania was limited to "24 oxen, 17 cows, 4 bulls, 8 year and vantage, 5 yearlings, 2 calves, 30 horses, mares and colts, 30 head of swine, 147 sheep."[16]

Further, from existing inventories and records, it appears that only enough small grain was grown to feed the domestic livestock. Haying seems to have been a principal occupation at the manor. Haying, however, was not done on planted fields, but by harvesting marsh grass growing wild on the lowlands of the property.

A neighborhood quarrel concerning haying at Morrisania seems worthy of relating. It involved Stony, or Stone Island, which has long since fallen victim to New York's land reclamation program. The island lay in Bronx Kill between the Westchester mainland and Little Barent's Island, now Randalls Island.

The trouble began in 1679 when the Colonel sent several Negroes in three canoes to the island to cut hay. When the Negroes were seen carrying away the hay and were asked who had given them permission to cut it, they replied that their master, Colonel Lewis Morris, had authorized it. When told to give up the hay, the Negroes said that they would fight to keep what they had cut.

Promptly, Daniel Tourneur, Cornelius Jansen and Laurens Jansen brought suit against the Colonel for trespass. Tourneur and the two Jansens claimed that they, as heirs, had been rightfully in possession of the island since 1663. The Colonel, however, claimed that it was included in his purchase of the Jonas Bronx property in 1668.

Tourneur and the Jansens won their trespass suit, whereupon they promptly brought suit in the New York courts to recover the value of the hay. The Colonel answered their suit by stating that if the claim was for hay taken off Stony Island, then the New York courts lacked jurisdiction over the matter, because the island was, as the Colonel claimed, under the jurisdiction of the Jamaica, Long Island courts. While this jurisdictional quarrel continued, Morris again sent his Negroes to the island to cut hay, whereupon Tourneur and the Jansens secured a warrant "giving warning to Colonel Lewis Morris, his agent, workmen and servants."[17]

Tourneur and the Jansens next appealed, by petition, to Governor Andros. In answer to the petition, Morris expressed his willingness, if necessary, to prove his right to the island in a court of proper jurisdiction, namely at Jamaica, Long Island. Andros took no action, and the matter rested for about two years while the Colonel continued to cut the hay on the island. In fact, when Tourneur tried to cut a crop of hay, he was forceably ejected from the island by the Colonel's men.

Tourneur and the Jansens then brought suit in the Jamaica courts, where the Colonel claimed the suit belonged. The matter came before the Court of Sessions there, during the next summer. Again, the verdict was in favor of Tourneur and the Jansens, but the Colonel promptly put in a plea of "Arrest of judgment," and the verdict was quashed.[18]

After many additional Morris maneuvers, the case was again brought to trial over five years and many hay cuttings after the original dispute was joined. As before, the Colonel lost the verdict. Yet, even in defeat, the Colonel displayed, at an advanced age of over seventy, all of the fight and tenacity, so typical of his younger years.

1. Diary 2:377.
2. Bolton 2:489 (1905 ed.).
3. Diary 2:11.
4. Ibid. 2:419; Bolton 2:opp. 490 (1905 ed.).
5. Harrisse.
6. Bolton 2:451 (1905 ed.).
7. Diary 2:419.
8. Bolton 2:300 (1905 ed.).
9. Smith, N.Y.
10. Bolton 2:289 (1905 ed.).
11. Ibid 2:294.
12. Ibid 2:294.
13. Flushing 1681, 8th mo., 12th day.
14. Hamm.
15. Bolton 2:299 (1905 ed.).
16. Ibid 2:299 (1905 ed.).
17. NY Col. Mss.; Riker 413 et seq.
18. Ibid.

17

Leisler
Antagonist

In February 1685, while Colonel Lewis Morris was serving in a dual capacity on the governing council of East New Jersey under Lawrie, and on the governing council of New York under Dongan, Charles II died, and his brother James, Duke of York, became King James II.

James had been very close to the New York-New Jersey situation, having been granted, in 1664, twenty-one years before his accession, all the land from the Delaware to the Connecticut River, plus what is presently Maine. Now, in James II, there was a King on the British throne who, having lost confidence in proprietary governments, would take action to bring all the land from Nova Scotia to the Delaware under direct royal control.

One of James' first moves to this end was to appoint a royal governor of "The Dominion of New England." For this post, James selected a man who had dedicated his later life to the proposition that all of the former domain in America of the Duke, now King, should be under one royal governor. The man chosen was Edmund Andros, now Sir Edmund Andros.

Although Andros would be residing in Boston, he would be closely in touch with his old friend, Lewis Morris. They would see each other often, and they would again participate in undertakings of mutual interest.

Within a short time, Andros gained control of all of the settlements down to the border of the Province of New York, and he extinguished all proprietary interests in that area. Now, there was a royal governor controlling the whole of New England with another royal governor, Thomas Dongan, in New York.

The Jersey proprietors became worried that their powers would soon be curtailed. Motivated by fear, internal strife, and economics, there were several rapid changes in New Jersey government. Then, the blow was struck for consolidation. Both East and West New Jersey proprietors had no other alternative than to surrender their rights to govern, which they did in April, 1688.[1] The proprietors, however, were permitted to retain their right to the land.

Further, Governor Dongan's commission as governor of New York was suspended in favor of Andros. Now, Andros ruled what he always hoped to rule, the domain from Nova Scotia to the Delaware. Representative government, where it had been so cherished, ceased to exist. Andros could, and did, impose his customs duty and other taxes as he saw fit throughout the area under his jurisdiction.

The stage was being set for Lewis Morris to participate in one of the most exciting dramas in colonial American history. The cast of characters included King James II, a Roman Catholic; Sir Edmund Andros, an Anglican; Colonel Lewis Morris, a Quaker; and Jacob Leisler, a German Protestant.

James II had married a Roman Catholic and had secretly joined the Roman Catholic Church almost fifteen years before he became King, although he continued to attend Anglican services for some time. By the time he ascended to the throne, the fact of James' Catholicism was publicly known, but not taken too seriously. It did not become a matter of concern to the Anglicans until James started invoking measures that appeared to protestant leaders to indicate that he aimed to make Roman Catholicism the dominant, if not the only, religion in England, whereupon a protestant succession became the object of his opponents.

After a long series of incidents, English Anglicans contacted William, Prince of Orange, living in Holland, who was a Protestant and had married King James' oldest daughter, Mary. William was invited to bring an invading army to England, which he agreed to do. The army landed in England on November 5, 1688, and on December 11, King James II fled to France.

On February 13, 1689, William and Mary were proclaimed King and Queen, and on April 4, Andros received word in Boston of the proclamation. On April 18, the people of Boston rose in revolt, and Governor Andros was seized and lodged in prison.

The principal charges against Andros were:

1. That he stifled the news of Prince William's landing in England.
2. That he made laws disruptive to the people.
3. That he levied taxes without consent of the people.
4. That he inflicted punishment on those who resisted the illegal taxes.
5. That he invaded the property of others.
6. That he supplied Indians with ammunition in time of war and encouraged them to make war on the English.[2]

In New Jersey, there was confusion and talk of revolt as well as agitation to return to proprietary government, although no actual outbreaks took place there.

In New York, the situation got very much out of hand. Jacob Leisler, a New York merchant, led a revolt there against what he called the "popish" government of James II and Governor Andros. He is said to have been chosen to lead the revolution because of his flat refusal to pay customs duties to a Roman Catholic tax collector named Plowman.

There may have been more to his refusal than his objection to Plowman. Leisler was an importer of wines from Europe. It had been Andros who had all but driven Leisler out of business in favor of Lewis Morris and other Barbadian merchants by imposing a heavy tax on wine imports while at the same time setting a very low rate on rum.[3]

A letter written on July 9, 1689 to Andros, who had now been in jail in Boston for three months, gives the chronology of the "Leisler Revolution." The letter to Andros was from Stephen Van Cortland, mayor of New York, and a member of the governing council of the Province of New York. In its opening, Van Cortland informed Andros that William Bickley, Lewis Morris' first servant, had sent word to him that he, Bickley, was leaving Westchester at high tide in the morning. Consequently, Van Cortland must hurry to finish the letter so that it could be carried, by Bickley, to Boston and secretly smuggled to Andros in jail.

Van Cortland went on to cover Leisler's doings as follows:

March 1: He learned of William, the Prince of Orange, landing in England.
April 26: He heard of the Revolution in Boston.
April 27: He learned of war with France.
April 30: He sent word to Albany to be on the alert for an invasion from the north by the French, supported by Indians.

May 4:   He learned of a revolt on Long Island.

May 31:   Captain Francis Nicholson, deputy governor in New York
           under Andros, in place of Dongan, warned magistrates
           and officers of possible rebellion in New York.

May 31:   A pro-Leisler demonstration was held in front of Jacob
           Leisler's house, and later, Henry Cuyler, on watch at Fort
           James, opened the gates and let Leisler and followers in.

June 3:   Leisler, in complete control, seized all records and letters
           of the government.

June 22:   A delegation from Connecticut headed by Major Gold
           came to New York to consult with Leisler. Gold had in
           hand the proclamation proclaiming William and Mary the
           new English Sovereigns.

June 24:   A proclamation confirming all protestants in office arrived
           in New York.

July 2:   Leisler appointed a Committee of Safety, and was in full
           control of the government of the Province of New York.[4]

Colonel Nicholas Bayard, head of the New York Militia, another member of the governing council of the Province of New York, clarified the visit of Major Gold from Connecticut by stating in his journal that on June 19, Major Gold was expected by land from Connecticut.[5] On the 20th, not having heard from Gold, Van Cortland and Bayard, with several gentlemen, went to meet Gold, but they did not see him.

Leisler knew of Mayor Van Cortland's journey for the purpose of meeting Gold and arranged for his son and one Sergeant Stoll to spy on the mayor. Young Leisler observed that when Van Cortland and Bayard tired of waiting for Gold, they went to Colonel Morris' at Morrisania.

Instead of meeting Van Cortland, Gold had proceeded to the Fort, where he showed Leisler the Proclamation for William and Mary, it being the first actual documentary evidence of it to be seen in New York. Leisler read it aloud to the people, using the instrument as a symbol—suggesting his closeness to William and Mary as compared to that of the Andros council, left waiting to meet Gold on the outskirts of town.

Leisler was not one to exercise his power from behind the scenes. He promptly assumed the title of "Lieutenant Governor and Commander in Chief.'' Since Leisler was in control of the fort, it was necessary for Andros' government to establish headquarters elsewhere. Morrisania, the home of Colonel Lewis Morris, was one of the designated places.[6] Leisler, being aware of this, descended on Morrisania with a raiding party. He also intercepted mail being forwarded to Andros from Morrisania.

Nicholas Bayard, in a published account of the revolution printed in London in 1690 (while the rebellion still raged), titled *A Modest Impartial Narrative*, stated: "the Publick Post Mr. John Perry setting out from the House of Colonel Lewis Morris towards Boston was not advanced on his way above a quarter of a mile before he was laid hold on by a warrant from our usurper Leysler."[7]

Relative to the same incident, in a letter from Leisler to the Bishop of Salisbury, Leisler stated: "By stopping a letter carried for Boston. . . [to Andros intercepted at the house of] Coll Morris. . . who is a quaker at convenient distance from New York: the said Morris hath entertained and countenanc'd that party [Andros] with great encouragements ever since the Revolucions: [I] have obtained severall letters whereby Your Lordshipp may perceive the horrible devices they [Andros and Morris] can invent. . . but when he [Morris] came before us he would not owne any of his writings which we can sufficiently prove upon him. . . . "[8]

Through intercepted letters and other methods Leisler tried to build a case to show that Andros was secretly a Catholic and against all Protestants. To bolster this claim, Leisler secured depositions from three men who alleged that an Indian, Sachem Wessicanow of Weskeskek, told each of the three, that prior to his being seized and thrown in jail, Andros had been in New York at the home of Lewis Morris.[9] There Andros and Morris were said to have met the chief, who was promised a considerable sum of wampum if he would raise a force of Indians that would join an intended French invasion from the north in order to kill all Protestants in New York and turn the territory over to Roman Catholic France. This was very inflamatory talk, and Lewis Morris was in great danger. There was just enough evidence that an attack might be made, to frighten the people into believing the story.

France was at war with England and many families from upper New York fled into New York City fearing an invasion. In fact, invasion by the French and Indians actually did take place that winter of 1690 with the burning of Schenectady, New York. Sixty men, women and children were massacred. The massacre was not for reasons alleged in the deposition against Morris and Andros, but rather in retaliation for an Indian raid from the American side against Montreal the summer before. Leisler, however, tried to make it appear to be the doing of Morris and Andros.[10]

While these charges were being made, there were several attempts by Andros to escape from jail in Boston. In one attempt, Andros disguised himself as a woman. A contemporary account stated ''on Friday last towards evening Sir Edmond Andros did attempt to make an escape in woman's apparel and passed two guards and was stopped at the third being discovered by his shoes; not having changed them.''[11]

Another time, Andros escaped to Rhode Island where he was to have been picked up by boat.[12] The boat did not arrive in time and Andros was recaptured and returned to Boston.

Even before he was lodged in the Boston jail, there had been an attempt by Andros to flee Boston in a vessel, which appeared off shore to rescue him.[13] However, the small boat sent ashore to pick him up was captured along with quantities of ''small arms, hand grenadoes, and a quantity of match.'' Andros then voluntarily went back into the fort.

Eventually, William and Mary sent word that Andros was to be brought to England to stand trial, and by February 1690, he was on his way. A trial was held and Andros was found to have committed no crime. By 1692, with continuing good fortune, Andros was made Governor of Virginia and Maryland.

Leisler held control of New York until March 20, 1691, when newly appointed Governor Slaughter's men took over Fort James and ''Bayard's chain was put on Leisler's legg.'' In other words, Leisler was arrested and put in leg irons by Colonel Nicholas Bayard, head of the militia prior to Leisler's rule. Leisler was subsequently tried, convicted, and executed. Thus, the first American Revolutionary War was ended.[14]

1. Smith NJ 211 note, 568.
2. Tracts.
3. Liquor Laws 113.
4. NYD 3:590–597.
5. Ibid: 599, 600, 601.
6. Ibid: 661, 662, 663.
7. Narrative 350.
8. NYD 3:656, 657.
9. Ibid: 659.
10. Pearson 237 et seq.; NYD 1:193.
11. Tracts.
12. Whitmore 32.
13. Tracts.
14. Leisler himself called it a "Revolucion." NYD 3:656, 657.

18

Severe Disciplinarian

Colonel Lewis Morris was in his late seventies at the conclusion of the Leisler Revolution. He had lived a strenuous life. He was in prison at least twice, for long periods. He was in many battles and was wounded at least once. He was ill for many years, possibly as a result of these experiences.[1] His first wife, Anne, had died, and in his old age, after being many years alone, he married his maid servant, Mary.[2] No known children were born to either marriage.

Time was running out for Colonel Lewis Morris. These were certainly reasons enough for him to be concerned about the disposition of his vast estates.

The Colonel's first act to this end was to make provisions for Lewis Morris, son of Thomas, now in his early thirties. Lewis had not become a Quaker, which concerned the Colonel. Nevertheless, the Colonel would provide for him, because as in the case of Lewis, son of Richard, he had been a ward of the Colonel from infancy.

Initially, the Colonel had purchased 300 acres in Middletown for Lewis, son of Thomas, then transferred title to the 300 acres to him in 1681, presumably when he became of age. Then, in 1688, the Colonel sold him, with certain limitations, three hundred and thirty acres at the end of Rumson Neck, New Jersey, having allowed him to live there for several years prior to that.[3] The next year the Colonel gave him the property outright and forgave other debts owed by Lewis to the Colonel. In gratitude Lewis stated: "Therefore [I, Lewis] am bound in duty to remain thankfully engaged unto him [the Colonel] forever and not only for the forementioned but also for many other kindness conferred on me by him from my Infancy too many to Enumerate here...."[4]

Next the Colonel made provisions for William Bickley, his first servant.[5] For a small consideration, the Colonel deeded to Bickley one thousand acres of land on the south side of the Monmouth River in West New Jersey, now Alloways Creek in Salem County, New Jersey.[6]

The Colonel seems to have done nothing more about disposing of his holdings for almost two years from the time he deeded the property to Bickley. The reason for this delay is quite understandable. The Colonel had intended to make his ward, Lewis Morris, son of his brother, Richard, his sole heir for the residue of his estate.[7] This had been virtually agreed upon with Richard, long ago. Now, something had happened that complicated matters. Lewis had run away from home. He was seventeen years old when he left, in late 1688 or early 1689.

The runaway's son, Robert Hunter Morris, many years later explained why his father had done so. He said Mary, Colonel Lewis' second wife, formerly his servant "used every means to set the old gentleman against his nephew that she and her poor relatives might share his fortune and . . . she so far prevailed as to make his life very uneasy and to avoid her Tyranny he ran away from his unkle traviled on foot to Virginia whence he went to Bermuda and so to Jamaica where he staid till his unkle learnt where he was and sent a vessel for him. He returned time enough to see his unkle alive and that was all for he died about a week after his arrival, having been ill for a long time . . . ."[8]

The Colonel died February 14, 1691, at Morrisania.[9]

His will had been written February 12, 1691, two days before his death and four or five days after young Lewis returned home.[10] The will had been prepared at Morrisania, and it was in the handwriting of William Bickley, the Colonel's first servant. The Colonel's signature was witnessed by five persons, probably domestics, identified by name only.[11]

Three days after the death of the Colonel, young Lewis appeared at Fort William Henry, formerly Fort James, before Major Richard Ingoldsby, with an inventory of the personal property belonging to the Colonel, which amounted to £4071:1:16.[12] Lewis swore to the correctness of the inventory, except for an error in addition. Up to this moment, Lewis had not seen the will, which was still in the hands of Bickley.[13]

Just one week after the Colonel's death, Mary Morris, the Colonel's wife, died.[14]

It was sometime shortly after Mary's death that young Lewis was told of certain erasures and alterations in the will.[15] The will, as altered, provided bequests in part as follows: It gave two-hundred and fifty acres in New Jersey to Thomas Webley, son of Walter Webley, Jr. To Lewis Morris, son of Thomas, to whom the Colonel had already given Passage Point on Rumson Neck, New Jersey, the will bequested one of the best mares in the woods and £20 New York currency. The will also made bequests of many slaves, one of them bequeathed to William Penn. It also gave £5 per annum "forever" to the Shrewsbury Meeting of Friends (Quakers) and £5 per annum "forever" to the New York Meeting of Friends.

Concerning young Lewis Morris, son of Richard, the will stated, "whereas I formerly intended to have made my nephew, Lewis Morris, son of my deceased brother, Richard Morris, my sole executor; his many and great miscarryages and disobedience toward me and my wife, and his causless absenting himself from my house, and adhering to and advizeing with those of bad life and conversation, contrary to my directions and example unto him, and for other reasons best known to my selfe, I do make and ordaine my dearly beloved wife, Mary Morris, sole executrix of this my last will and testament. . . ."[16]

Then the will provided bequest to "nephew Lewis" of the plantation and iron works at Tinton, New Jersey together with everything there, including slaves; the land and meadows at Matinecock, Oyster Bay Long Island; and several small items of silver; plus one small cabinet "sealed up" in which were four necklaces, three or four jewels set in gold, etc. In addition, he was to have a negro, Bess, and her children, the jewels and negro previously belonging to Lewis' father, Richard.

The will also gave "nephew Lewis" some small silver items to replace those "that are lost and supposed to be embezzled by Walter Webley" during the Dutch occupation; and £20 in silver (current rate at New York) plus ten guineas.

Then, defiantly, is added that despite "any pretence or right from his father [Richard] aforementioned whether by partnership with or purchase or anyway else," he, Lewis, shall quietly and peaceably acquiesce and submit himself wholly and absolutely unto everything mentioned, or to be mentioned in the will, or even that which is given will be revoked and given to Mary, the Colonel's wife, except £10 New York currency.

"Unto dearly beloved wife Mary Morris, her heirs and assigns forever," the Colonel bequeathed the remainder of his estate, which included Morrisania, and the house in New York City.

Lastly, the Colonel appointed his "trusty friends," Richard Jones and Miles Foster of New York, John Bowne of Flushing, William Richardson of Westchester, Richard Hartshorne and John Hance of Monmouth County and William Bickley of Westchester "executors in trust and overseers to see this my will punctually performed and fulfilled. . . ."

The hearing in connection with the probation of the will was held before Governor Slaughter and his council.[17] At the hearing, Lewis Morris, who was five months short of his twentieth birthday, revealed for the first time the legal talent that would make him a member of the Court of Common Right and a member of the governing council of East New Jersey by age twenty-one.

Lewis charged before the governor and council that the will had been altered by William Bickley, the Colonel's first servant, in conspiracy with Mary, the Colonel's wife, now deceased, who formerly had been one of the Colonel's servants. The will had been altered, Lewis said, in such a way as to deprive him of a large part of the estate. One specific alteration, claimed by Lewis, was that the words "her heirs and assignes forever" had been inserted in place of erased words, which probably gave her only a life estate in Morrisania.[18]

It was also charged that while the Colonel lay dying and Lewis was away in Jamaica with "his life and return uncertain—[Bickley and Mary were] expecting to divide between them what was left." It was alleged, further, that Bickley and Mary had "secreted great sums of money and other valuable effects."[19]

To bolster his case, Lewis first showed erasures and interlineations in the will, and produced witnesses to the will who claimed they had no knowledge of the changes and erasures which were made. In cross-examination, it was revealed that Bickley knew of the erasures but could not, or did not, say for what reason they were made, although both the will and changes were in Bickley's hand.[20]

Then Lewis played a trump card. He produced evidence that William Bickley, at about the time the will was being drawn, had purchased a play, "The Orphan," by Thomas Otway.[21] Otway was a contemporary poet and playwright, whose play portrayed a deceitful and grasping villain who tried to steal the estate of an innocent orphan. The first two heroic couplets of the epilogue, spoken by the orphan, read as follows:[22]

"You've seen one orphan ruin'd here, and I
May be the next, if Old Acasto dye:
Should it prove so, I'd fain amongst you find,
Who 'tis would to the Fatherless be kind."

The purpose here is not to retry the case of Lewis Morris versus Lewis Morris. The governor of New York and his council tried it in 1691 and found in favor of young Lewis Morris by refusing to admit the will to probate and by appointing young Lewis administrator of the Colonel's estate.[23]

To the most casual observer, however, it must be evident that the Colonel was very displeased with Lewis for his "great miscarryages and disobedience . . . and adhering to and advizeing with those of bad life and conversation contrary to my directions and example unto him . . . ." What is more, Lewis did not try to explain away those harsh words nor claim that they were added by Bickley. It seems fair to ask why the Colonel was so upset with Lewis' behavior?

First, it must be remembered that the Colonel, almost from the day of his conversion to Quakerism back in the 1650s or 1660s was a "severe Quaker." His first wife was a Quaker; his second was also. His first servant, William Bickley, was a Quaker; his close friends were Quakers; the bequests in his will were mainly to relatives and Quakers; the overseers named in his will were all Quakers.

As might be expected, his nephew and ward, Lewis, son of Richard, was brought up a Quaker. Young Lewis' education first had been under the direction of Hugh Cowperthwait, a Quaker teacher from Long Island.[24] After the Colonel moved from New York to East New Jersey, young Lewis became "the Scholar" of George Keith, then a Quaker teacher and preacher, in addition to being surveyor general of East New Jersey.[25]

It could have been during this period, when George Keith himself was questioning the "God from within" doctrine of the Quakers, and was about to turn Anglican, that young Lewis may have been weaned away from his Quaker teachings and examples.[26]

Notwithstanding, all the "direction and example unto him," as the Colonel phrased it in his will, young Lewis became an Anglican—as he was born. In fact, he, like George Keith, became a leading Quaker critic and adversary. This was evident almost from the day of his uncle's death, and continued until his own death, some fifty years later.[27]

In his lifetime, young Lewis Morris participated in religion (albeit a different one) with the same zeal that his uncle had shown in his. He became an outstanding lawyer, judge, and high government official as had his uncle. He became an excellent sailor and navigator as his uncle had been. He even became a colonel and took on the name "Colonel Lewis Morris," which had been his uncle's trademark for years. Thus, there appears to have emerged upon the early 18th century scene, a new Lewis Morris, strikingly like the old one.

1. Morris: RHM 1763 Corres.
2. Ibid. Mary was probably from Barbados and was in some way related to a Peter Bishop, NY Col. Mss. 38:58, indexed p. 220.
3. Tinton: 3.30.1688 and 4.15.1689 Deeds; 1681 confirmation as "first purchaser" from year 1670. Stillwell 4:34.
4. Morris: 4.24.1689 Release. For a map showing the location of the Rumson Neck property and adjacent properties, see *Sandy Hook and the Land of the Navesink* by Samuel S. Smith, 1963, p.26.
5. Riker 444.
6. Salem Deed Book 4:162. The property had come to the Colonel from William Penn and the other executors of the will of John Fenwick, in exchange for a previously granted one thousand acres on the Delaware River in the Finn's Point-Salem Cove, New Jersey, area. This grant called for rent at the rate of two bushels of winter wheat a year for the entire tract. This rent rate carried over in the Bickley Transfer. Salem Deed Book B: 10, 86, 113.
7. Bolton 2:284; Papers 325 lines 4–15.
8. Morris RHM 1763 Corres.
9. JFHS 10:26.
10. Bolton 2:290 et seq.
11. Papers 323 line 22, 23.
12. NYHS Mss. 1691.
13. Papers 323 line 30; ibid: 325 line 11, 12.
14. JFHS 10:26.
15. Papers 323 line 32.
16. Bolton 2:290 et seq.
17. NY Wills 1:180, 181.
18. Papers 323 line 28, 30.
19. Morris RHM 1763 Corres.
20. Papers 324 lines 9, 10; Ibid 321 lines 2, 3.
21. Papers 324 lines 36, 37.
22. Otway.
23. NY Wills 1:180, 181.
24. Smith NY 125, 126; Cox 161; Monnette 811, 812.
25. SPG: Keith 1702 Letter, Guide 196, 197; Christ Church 7.
26. Miles Foster, one of the Quaker administrators selected by the Colonel, defected to the Anglicans shortly after the will was admitted to probate. Foster and young Lewis successfully fought the payment of bequests to the two Quaker meetings.
27. Flushing; Papers 8, 9, 296.

Bibliography

A.B. *A brief Relation of the beginning and ending of the troubles in Barbados*, A.B., a diligent observer of the times, London, 1653. (British Museum E 708).

Acts *Acts of Barbados 1643-1762*, London, 1764.

Akerly *The Morris Manor*, Lucy D. Akerly, New York, 1916.

America *American New World Empires*, John Ogilby, London, 1671.

Analytical *Collections of N.J. Historical Society Analytical Index to Colonial Documents of N.J., in State Papers Office, England, 1649-1799*, New York, 1858.

Andrews *The Colonial Period of American History*, Charles McLean Andrews, New Haven, 1934-38.

Applegate *Early Courts and Lawyers of Monmouth County*, John S. Applegate, 1911.

Baker *George and Margaret Fox*, W. King Baker, London.

Barb. Wills *Barbados Copied Wills*, Barbados, B.W.I.

Besse *A Collection of The Sufferings of The People Called Quakers*, Joseph Besse, London, 1753.

Bolton *A History of the County of Westchester*, Robert Bolton, Jr., New York, 1848. (also 1905 ed. as noted).

Bradney *The History of Monmouthshire*, Joseph Alfred Bradney, 1907-1932, London.

Britannica *The Encyclopedia Britannica*.

Br. Mus. The British Museum: Manuscript Division, London, England.

Brodhead *History of State of New York*, John Romeyn Brodhead, 1853.

Bugg *The Finishing Stroke*, Francis Bugg, London, 1712.

Cadbury *Annual Catalogue of George Fox's Papers*, Henry J. Cadbury, Phila. and London, 1939.

Camden "A Briefe Journall or a Succinct and True Relation of the Most Remarkable Passages Observed in the Voyage Undertaken by Captaine William Jackson to the Westerne Indies or Continent of America anno Domini 1642." Sloane mss. (British Museum), 793 or 894 —otherwise titled "Mercurius Americanus," author unknown. Printed in *Camden Miscellany* vol. XIII, Camden Third Series, Vol. XXXIV, London 1924.

Caribbeana *Caribbeana*, London, 1st issue, 1910.

Christ *History of Christ Church*, Shrewsbury, New Jersey, (Privately printed by James Steen, 1902).

CO Colonial Records, Public Record Office, London, England.

Cooks *Old Matinecock*, George William Cooks, Locust Valley, 1910.

Council Minutes of The Common Council of The City of New York, 1675-1776.

Cox *Quakerism in the City of New York 1657-1930*, J. M. Cox, Jr., 1930.

CSPC Calendar of State Papers, Great Britain, Public Record Office, London. (Colonial Series).

CSPD Calendar of State Papers, Great Britain, Public Record Office, London. (Domestic Series).

DAB *Dictionary of American Biography*.

117

Danckaerts *A Journal of a Voyage to New York 1679-80*, Jasper Danckaerts [Dankers] and Peter Sluyter, Brooklyn, 1867.

Davis *The Cavaliers and Roundheads of Barbados*, N. Darnell Davis, Georgetown, Br. Guiana, 1887. (Also an 1883 ed.)

Diary *Diary and Letters of Gouverneur Morris*, Anne Carey Morris, 1888.

Flushing Flushing Monthly Meeting (mss.) First Volume of Minutes 1671-1703, Friends Religious Soc. New York City.

Foster *A Briefe Relation of the Late Horrid Rebellion on Barbados*. Nicholas Foster, London, 1650.

Fox *The Journal of George Fox*, Norman Penney, London, 1911.

GMNJ *Genealogical Magazine of New Jersey*, Newark, N.J.

Guide *Guide to Manuscripts Relating to American History in British Depositories*. Library of Congress, 1946.

Hague *Memorial of the Courts of Great Britain and France Relative to the West Indies*, 1756.

Hamm *Famous Families of New York*, Margherita A. Hamm, 1901.

Harlow *A History of Barbados 1625-1685*, Vincent T. Harlow, Oxford, 1926.

Harrisse *De Manatus op de Noort Riuier*, original 1639, copy made ca. 1660-1665 by Vingboons, Harrisse Atlas, Library of Congress.

Hatfield *History of Elizabeth, New Jersey*, Rev. Edwin F. Hatfield, New York, 1868.

I.S. *A Briefe Journal of the late Proceedings . . . till June 24, 1655*, by I.S. (an eye witness), London, 1655.

JFHS *Journal Friends Historical Society*, London, England.

Journal *Journal, The Barbados Museum and Historical Society*, Barbados, B.W.I.

Judicial *The Judicial and Civil History of New Jersey*, John Whitehead, Boston, 1897.

Kemmerer *Path to Freedom, 1703-1776*. Donald E. Kemmerer, Princeton, 1940.

Land Papers *Calendar of N.Y. Colonial Manuscripts, indorsed Land Papers, 1643-1803*, Albany, 1864.

L and S *The Grants and Concessions etc. of Province of N.J.*, Aaron Leaming and Jacob Spicer, Philadelphia, 1752.

Leeds *The Mystery of Fox-Craft*, Daniel Leeds, New York, 1705.

Lefferts *Descendants of Lewis Morris of Morrisania*, Elizabeth Morris Lefferts, N.D.

Lereck *A True relation of the late reduction of the Isles of Scilly*, Jos. Lereck, London, 1651. (British Museum Catalogued E638).

Lindsay *William Claiborne of Virginia*, John D. Lindsay, New York, 1917.

Liquor Laws *Colonial Liquor Laws*, G. Thomann, New York, 1887.

Lucas *Minutes of Council of Barbados*, copied by Dr. Lucas, Barbados Public Library, B.W.I.

Manchester Manchester Papers, 1605-1647, Public Record Office, London.

McCormick *Experiment in Independence New Jersey 1781-1789*, Richard P. McCormick, New Brunswick, 1950.

Md. Hist. Mag. *Maryland Historical Magazine*.

Mercurius *Mercurius Politicus*, John Milton and Marchamount Needham, London. (Began publication June 1650).

Miller *The Minutes of the Board of Proprietors of East Jersey, 1685-1705*, George J. Miller, New York, 1949-1960.

Mirror *Mariner's Mirror*, Cambridge Univ. Press, London.

Monnette *First Settlers of ye Plantations of Piscataway and Woodbridge . . . 1664-1714*, Orra E. Monnette, Los Angeles, 1930-35.

Morris Morris Papers, Rutgers University, New Brunswick, N.J.

NAR *The Record of New Netherland 1653-1674*, Berthold Fernow, 1897.

Narrative *Narratives of the Insurrection 1675-1690*, New York, 1915.

Nicholas *Nicholas Papers* (Sir Edward) George F. Warner, ed., 1886.

Nickalls *The Journal of George Fox*, J. L. Nickalls, Cambridge, 1952.

Newton *The Colonizing Activities of the English Puritans*, Arthur Percival Newton, Oxford, 1914.

NJA *New Jersey Archives*—Published under sponsorship of State of New Jersey.

NY Col. Mss. New York Colonial Manuscripts, New York State Library, Albany, N.Y. (Bound in 1919, Calendar, Edmund B. O Callaghan, ed., 1866).

NYD *Documents relative to The Colonial History of New York....* Albany, N.Y., Edmund B. O'Callaghan and Berthold Fernow, eds., 15 vols., 1853-1887.

NYG&BR *New York Genealogical and Biographical Record,* New York, N.Y.

NYHS Mss. The New York Historical Society, manuscripts collection, New York, N.Y.

NY Wills *Collection of New York Historical Society,* New York, N.Y.

Oldmixon *History of the British Settlements in America,* John Oldmixon, 1708.

Otway *The Orphan,* Thomas Otway, (1652-1685).

Oyster Bay *Oyster Bay New York Town Record,* New York, 1916.

Pa. Mag. *The Pennsylvania Magazine of History and Biography,* Phila., Pa.

Papers *The Papers of Lewis Morris 1738-1746,* N.J. Historical Society Collection, New York, 1852.

Pearson *A History of The Schenectady Patent,* Jonathan Pearson, Albany, 1883.

Plantagenet *A Description of the Province of New Albion, etc.* Beauchamp Plantagenet, 1648.

Penn Papers Penn Papers (mss.) Friends Reference Library, 12 Bishops Gate, Without E. C. London.

PNJHS *Proceedings New Jersey Historical Society,* Newark, N.J.

Powell *The Letters of Robert Blake,* J. R. Powell. London MDCCCCXXXVIII (Publication of Naval Records Society LXXVI).

PRO Public Record Office, London, England.

Riker *Harlem, Its Origin and early Annals,* James Riker, New York, 1881.

Salem Deeds Salem Deed Books, State Capitol Building, Trenton, N.J. (Op. cit. 1 NJA 21).

Schomburgk *The History of Barbados,* Sir Robert H. Schomburgk, London, 1847.

Scot *The Model of Government of the Province of East New Jersey,* George Scot, Edinburgh, 1685.

Sea Jnl. Admiral William Penn's Sea Journal to the West Indies, Dec. 25, 1654-Sept. 4, 1655, National Maritime Museum, London (Catalogued Wyn/10/2).

Severall *Severall Proceedings in Parliament,* printed for Robert Ibbitson. London, 17th Century.

Shilstone *The Bajan and South Caribbean,* Bridgetown, Barbados. (Shilstone Article).

Sloane Sloane Manuscripts, The British Museum, London. Collection of Sir Hans Sloane.

Smith, N. J. *The History of New Jersey,* Samuel Smith, Burlington, N.J. 1765.

Smith, N. Y. *The History of the Province of New York,* William Smith, London, 1757.

Special *A perfect Diurnal of some Passages and Proceedings in relation to the Armies in England, Ireland and Scotland.* From Monday July 21 to Monday July 28, 1651. Printed by F. Leach and F. Griffin in Old Baily, London. (British Museum Catalogue No. 786).

SPG Society for the Propogation of the Gospel in Foreign Parts. (Microfilm records in Library of Congress, Washington, D.C.).

Stearns *Thirty Dunstable Families,* Edgar S. Stearns, Boston, 1911.

Stillwell *Historical and Genealogical Miscellany,* John E. Stillwell, M.D. New York, 1916.

Stokes *The Iconography of Manhattan Island, 1498-1909.* I.N.P. Stokes, New York, 1918.

Swarthmore Swarthmore Mss. Library Society of Friends, Friends House Euston, London, N.W.I. (Microfilm copies Swarthmore College, Swarthmore, Pa.)

Thompson *History of Long Island,* Benjamin F. Thompson, New York, 1918.

Thurloe Thurloe's [John] State Papers, London, 1742.

Tinton Tinton Iron Works (Manuscript Collection) Monmouth County Historical Association, Freehold, N.J.

Tracts *The Tracts and other Papers of the Colonies,* collected by Peter Force, Washington, 1846.

Valentine *History of The City of New York,* David T. Valentine, New York, 1853.

Venables *The Narrative of General Venables,* F. A. Firth, ed., London, 1900.

Whitehead *East Jersey under The Proprietary Governments,* Wm. A. Whitehead, 1875, revised edition.

Whitmore *A Memoir of Sir Edmund Andros KNT,* Wm. Henry Whitmore, Boston. 1868.

Winthrop *History of New England from 1630-1649,* John Winthrop, Boston, 1825.

FOUR GENERATIONS OF MORRISES IN AMERICA

1 Lewis Morris
b. ca. 16l3
d. 2.14. 1690/91
m1. ca. 1637
    Ann Barton (widow)
m2. Mary
d. ca. 2.21. 1690/91

2 Richard Morris
b. ca. 1616
d. 1672
m. 8.17.1669
    Sarah Poole
d. 1672

3 (sister) prob. Mary
b. ca. 1614
d. before 1672
m. Walter Webley
d. 1672

4 Lewis Morris
b. 10.15.1671
d. 5.21.1746
m. lic. 11.3.1691
    Isabella Graham
b. 6.3.1672-73
d. 4.6.1752

— 5 Walter Webley Jr.
    b. ca. 1640

— 6 Edward Webley
    alive 1698

— 7 Mary Morris
    m. Vincent Pearse

— 8 Euphemnia Morris
    m. Matthew Norris

— 9 Anne Morris
    m. Edward Antill II

— 10 Elizabeth Morris
    m. Anthony White

— 11 Margaret Morris
    m. Isaac Willet

— 12 Arabella Morris
    m. James Graham

— 13 Lewis Morris
    m1. Tryntje Staats
    m2. Sarah Gouverneur

— 14 Robert Hunter Morris

— 15 John Morris

— 16 James Morris
    m. Isabella

— 17 Isabella Morris
    m. Richard Ashfield

— 18 Sarah Morris
    m. Michael Kearny

— 19-22 four died young

23 Thomas Webley —
    m. Audria West

24 Mary Webley —
    m. Joseph West

*Denotes line carried forward else-
where by number.

Note: Although we have published
only the first four generations of
Morrises in America, information is
available on later generations by
writing Morris Genealogies Box 116
Monmouth Beach, N.J. 07750.

122

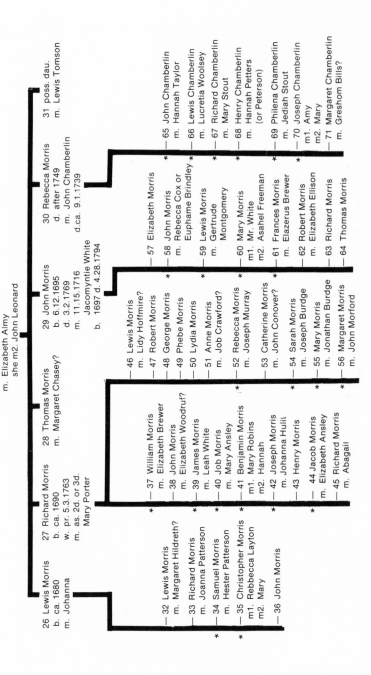

25 Lewis Morris
   (son of Thomas)
   b. prob. 1660 d. 1695
   m. Elizabeth Almy
   she m2. John Leonard

26 Lewis Morris
   b. ca. 1680
   m. Johanna

27 Richard Morris
   b. ca. 1690
   w. pr. 5.3.1763
   m. as. 2d. or 3d.
      Mary Porter

28 Thomas Morris
   m. Margaret Chasey?

29 John Morris
   b. 6.12.1695
   d. 3.2.1769
   m. 11.15.1716
      Jacomyntie White
   b. 1697 d. 4.28.1794

30 Rebecca Morris
   d. after 1749
   m. John Chamberlin
   d.ca. 9.1.1739

31 poss. dau.
   m. Lewis Tomson

   * 32 Lewis Morris
        m. Margaret Hildreth?

   * 33 Richard Morris
        m. Joanna Patterson

   * 34 Samuel Morris
        m. Hester Patterson

   * 35 Christopher Morris
        m1. Rebbecca Layton
        m2. Mary

   36 John Morris

   *— 37 William Morris
         m. Elizabeth Brewer

   — 38 John Morris
        m. Elizabeth Woodruf?

   *— 39 James Morris
         m. Leah White

   *— 40 Job Morris
         m. Mary Ansley

   *— 41 Benjamin Morris
         m1. Mary Robins
         m2. Hannah

   — 42 Joseph Morris
        m. Johanna Hulit

   *— 43 Henry Morris

   — 44 Jacob Morris
        m. Elizabeth Ansley

   — 45 Richard Morris
        m. Abagail

   — 46 Lewis Morris
        m. Lidy Hoffmire?

   — 47 Robert Morris

   — 48 George Morris

   — 49 Phebe Morris

   — 50 Lydia Morris

   — 51 Anne Morris
        m. Job Crawford?

   *— 52 Rebecca Morris
         m. Joseph Murray

   — 53 Catherine Morris
        m. John Conover?

   *— 54 Sarah Morris
         m. Joseph Burdge

   *— 55 Mary Morris
         m. Jonathan Burdge

   *— 56 Margaret Morris
         m. John Morford

   — 57 Elizabeth Morris

   *— 58 John Morris
         m. Rebecca Cox or
            Euphame Brindley

   *— 59 Lewis Morris
         m. Gertrude
            Montgomery

   *— 60 Mary Morris
         m1. Mr. White
         m2. Asahel Freeman

   *— 61 Frances Morris
         m. Elazerus Brewer

   — 62 Robert Morris
        m. Elizabeth Ellison

   — 63 Richard Morris

   — 64 Thomas Morris

   *— 65 John Chamberlin
         m. Hannah Taylor

   *— 66 Lewis Chamberlin
         m. Lucretia Woolsey

   *— 67 Richard Chamberlin
         m. Mary Stout

   *— 68 Henry Chamberlin
         m. Hannah Petters
            (or Peterson)

   *— 69 Philena Chamberlin
         m. Jediah Stout

   *— 70 Joseph Chamberlin
         m1. Amy
         m2. Mary

   — 71 Margaret Chamberlin
        m. Greshom Bills?

9. Anne Morris
b. 4.3.1706
w.pr. 11.20. 1781
m. as his 2d.
6.10.1739
Edward Antill II
b. 6.17.1701
d. 8.15.1770

children:

Sarah Antill
m. Lt. Col. John Morris (nat.ch. of 15)

Lt. Col. Edward Antill III m. Charlotte Riverein

Maj. John Antill
m1. Margaret Colden
m2. Jane Colden

Dr. Lewis Antill
m. Alice Colden

Isabella Graham Antill m1.Rev. Robert McKean
m2. Mr. McNeil or McNeal

Mary Antill
m. Richard Cochran

---

10. Elizabeth Morris
b. 4.3.1712
w.pr. 8.30.1784
m. 12.14.1741
Col. Anthony White
b. 10.28.1717
d. 6.19.1787

children:

Isabella White

Johanna Kelsall White m.
Col. John Bayard as his 3d.

Euphemia Morris White m. Gov. William Paterson of N.J. as his 2d.

Lt. Col. Anthony Walton White
m. Margaret Ellis

---

12. Arabella Morris
(widow by 1767)
m. 11.30.1738
James Graham
b. ca. 1704
d. 6.24.1767

children:

James Graham

Augustine Graham
m. Mary Willett Van Ranst

Lewis Graham

Capt. Charles Graham

Col. Morris Graham

John Graham
m. Julia Ogden

Arabella Graham

Isabella Graham
m. Jonathan Landon

---

13. Lewis Morris
b. 9.23.1698
d. 7.3.1762
ml. 3.17.1723
Tryntje (Catherine) Staats
b. 4.4.1697
d. 3.11.1731
m2. 11.3.1746
Sarah Gouverneur
b. 10.14.1714
d. 1.14.1786

children:

Mary Morris m. Thomas Lawrence Jr.

Lewis Morris
m. Mary Walton

Maj. Staats Long Morris m. Catherine Gordon

Richard Morris
m. Sarah Ludlow

Isabella Morris m. Rev. Isaac Wilkins

Sarah Morris m. Vincent Pearse Ashfield (son of 17)

Gouverneur Morris m. Ann Cary Randolph

Euphemia Morris m. Col. Samuel Ogden

Catherine Morris
m. Philip Ashfield

---

14. Robert Hunter Morris
b. ca. 1700
d. 1.27.1764

children:

Robert Morris
(nat. ch. supposed
by Elizabeth Stogdale)

Mary Morris
(nat. ch. supposed
by Elizabeth Stogdale)
m. Dr. James Boggs

---

15. John Morris

children:

Lt. Col. John Morris
(nat. ch.) m.
Sarah Antill
(dau. of 9)

Ann Morris
(nat. ch.)

17 Isabella Morris
b. 1705
d. 4.25.1741
m. 1723
   Richard Ashfield
b. 12.16.1695
d. 1742

children:

Lewis Ashfield m.
Elizabeth Redford

Richard Ashfield
(d. young)

Mary (Molly) Ashfield

Isabella Ashfield
m. Samuel Hunt

Patience Ashfield

Richard Ashfield
(d. young)

Vincent Pearse
Ashfield
m. Sarah Morris
(dau. of 13)

---

18 Sarah Morris
b. 1695-97
d. 5.29.1736
m. 1715 as his 3d.
   Michael Kearny
b. 1669
d. 5.7.1741

children:

Isabella Kearny

Mary Kearny m1.
Andrew Van Horne
m2. John Martin

Sarah Kearny

Euphemia Arabella
Kearny m.
Henry Leonard

Capt. Michael Kearny

Graham Kearny m.
Rev. Samuel Cooke

---

23 Thomas Webley
b. ca. 1660
d. 1702/3
m. Audria West
b. 3.6.1749

children:

Ann Webley m.
Richard Chambers

Catherine Webley
m. Philip Edwards

John Webley m.
Elizabeth Wooley?

Mary Webley

Audria Webley

---

24 Mary Webley
m. 1692
   Joseph West
d. 1715

children:

Webley West

Dr. Stephen West
m. Sarah Lippencott?

Joseph West

3 daus.

34 Samuel Morris
w.pr. 3.28.1780
m.   5.14.1740
     Hester Patterson

children:

Johanna Morris
m. William Taylor

Isaac Morris

Amariah Morris
m. Sarah Clayton

James Morris
m. Lydia Patterson

Robert P. Morris
m1. Content Dunham
m2. Mary Cooper

Zephaniah Morris
m. Mary Daws

John Morris

Elisha Morris

---

35 Christopher Morris
     (supposed son of 26)
w.pr. 6.17.1801
m1.lic. 5.1.1742
     Rebecca Layton
m2. before 1801
     Mary

children:

Mary Morris
m. Mr. Giberson

Ann Morris
m. Mr. Trout

Catherine Morris
m. Mr. DeBow

(prob.) William Morris
m. Martha Vaughn

---

37 William Morris
w.pr. 10.10.1782
m.   10.10.1739
     Elizabeth Brewer
     or Brower

children:

Adam Morris

Lydia Morris
m. John Warden

Phebe Morris

William Morris

Mary Morris
m. Peter Patterson

Richard Morris
m. Mary Throckmorton

Joel Morris
m. Rebecca Stillwell

Benjamin Morris
m. Abagail

---

39 James Morris
w.pr. 3.18.1769
m.lic. 7.18.1753
     Leah White

children:

Amos Morris
m. Lydia

Joel White Morris

2 daus.

---

40 Job Morris
w.pr. 8.25.1786
m.lic. 5.17.1760
     Mary Ansley
     (of William)

children:

James Morris
m1. Ann Jackson
m2. Elizabeth Curtis?

Zilpha Morris
m. Henry Williams

Mary Morris
m. Abram Sanders

Lydia Morris
m. Abel Ansley
   (of Thomas)

Rebecca Morris
m. Hugh Jackson

---

41 Benjamin Morris
w.pr. 1.29.1812
m1.lic. 12.2.1763
     Mary Robins
m2. Hannah

children:

Ezekial Morris
m. Nancy Robins

Ann Morris
m. Ezekial Robbins

Samuel Morris

Caleb Morris

Elisha Morris
m2. Deborah Burges

Mary (Molley) Morris

Deborah Morris

Sarah Morris

42 Joseph Morris
w.pr. 4.2.1763
m.lic. 8.2.1755
Johanna Hulit

children:

John Morris

Mary Morris
m. Benjamin White

Joseph Morris

William Morris?

44 Jacob Morris
w.pr. 9.23.1767
m. 2.13.1765
Elizabeth Ansley

children:

Jacob Morris
m. Judith Smith

child (posthumous)

52 Rebecca Morris
under 18 in 1762
m. Joseph Murray
d. 6.8.1780

children:

William Murray
m. Anna Schenck

James Murray
m. Alice

Joseph Murray
m. Mary D'Orsay

dau. m.
Mr. Havens

54 Sarah Morris
m. Joseph Burdge

children:

Jacob Burdge
m. Judith Smith

Samuel Burdge

55 Mary Morris
m.lic. 11.14.1746
Jonathan Burdge

children:

Joseph Burdge

Jonathan Burdge

(poss) Richard Burdge
m. Charity

56 Margaret Morris
m. John Morford
b. ca. 1715
d. 1739

children:

Garret Morford

Mary Morford
m. David Ketchum

Rebecca Morford
m. Jeremiah Horner

58 John Morris
b. 9.29.1724
d. 5.22.1789
m. Rebecca Cox
or Euphame Brindley

children:

John Morris

59 Lewis Morris
b. 7.17.1726
m. Gertruydt
(Gertrude) Montgomery
b. 10.27.1741

children:

Charles A. Morris
m. Catherine Van Antwerp

James Lawrence Morris
m. Abigail Tilton

Fanny Morris

Lewis Morris

Robert Morris
m. Elizabeth Monell

Ann Morris

Leah Morris

60 Mary Morris
b. 4.23.1730
d. 6.1.1806
m1. Mr. White
m2. lic. 12.7.1757
Asahel (Essec) Freeman

children:

Deborah White

Morris Freeman

Marssey Freeman

Ledia Freeman

Richard Freeman

Essec Freeman

Anne Freeman

James Freeman

61 Frances Morris
b. 2.15.1732/33
d. 2.27.1807
m.lic. 6.25.1755
   Elazerus Brewer
   (Brouwer)
b. 6.23.1731
d. 3.31.1820

children:

John Brewer
m. Constant Hulet

Adam Brewer

Aaron Robins Brewer
m. Elizabeth Cooper

Mary Brewer
m. William Matthews

Deborah Brewer
m. Amor Cook

George Brewer
m1. Rebecca Schenck
m2. Lydia Hulet

Elizabeth Brewer
m. James Van Kirk or Verbeck

---

65 John Chamberlin
b.ca 1712
d. 3.15.1783
m.ca. 1738?
   Hannah Taylor
b.ca 1720?
d. 6.30.1807

children:

Joseph Chamberlin
m2. Grace Randolph
m. Rebecca? Chamberlin
m. Mr. Mount

Ann Chamberlin
m. Joshua Ely

Elizabeth Chamberlin
m. Joseph Cox

Margaret Chamberlin
m. Matthias Mount?

John Chamberlin
m. Rebecca Mount

Lewis Chamberlin
m. Mary Mount

Enoch Chamberlin
m. Rachel Mount

---

66 Lewis Chamberlin
b.ca 1714
d. 5.3.1772
m. Lucretia Woolsey
d. 1.15.1812

children:

William Chamberlin
m1. Elizabeth Ten Broeck
m2. Anne Park
m3. Margaret Park
m4. Anne Marie Kemble
   Sarah Chamberlin
John Chamberlin
m. Mary Stout
Hannah Chamberlin
m. Daniel Wolverton
Rebecca Chamberlin
m. James Slack
Lucretia Chamberlin
Elizabeth Chamberlin
m. Derrick Hoagland
Lewis Chamberlin
m1. Mary Hagaman
m2. Sarah Fisher
m3. Ann Fisher
Anne Chamberlin
m. Derrick Sutphen
Uriah Chamberlin
m. Mary Pipenger or Sarah Pettinger
Rachel Chamberlin
m. Dr. John Andrew

---

67 Richard Chamberlin
b.ca. 1723
d.ca 11.1789
m. Mary Stout
   (dau. of Freegift)
b.ca. 1730?
d. after 1790

children:

John Chamberlin
Stout Chamberlin
Freegift Chamberlin
Amy Chamberlin
m. William Carpenter?
Amelia Chamberlin
m. David Kerr?
Premets Chamberlin

---

68 Henry Chamberlin
b. 6.19.1725
d. 10.15.1781
m. Hannah Petters or Peterson
b. 1.27.1727
d. 6.21.1815

children:

Jacob Chamberlin
Lewis Chamberlin
John Chamberlin
Godfrey Chamberlin
m. Mercy Moore
Mary Chamberlin
m. Amos Dey?
Noah Chamberlin
Maraba Chamberlin
Anna Chamberlin
Henry Chamberlin
Margaret Chamberlin
David Chamberlin
m. Mrs. Anne (Gaston) Holton
Sarah Chamberlin

128

69 Philena Chamberlin
b.ca. 1728
m.lic. 1.13.1744/45
      Jediah Stout
      (son of Freegift)
b.ca. 1726?

children:

Rebecca Stout
Ann Stout
Jediah Stout
and others

70 Joseph Chamberlin
b.ca. 1732
d. 4.16.1816
m1. Amy
b.ca. 1729
d. 5.1.1784
m2. Mary

children:

John Chamberlin
m. Eleanor Gray
Joseph Chamberlin

Amy Chamberlin
m. Peter Ten Broeck
David Chamberlin
m. Elizabeth

Clayton Chamberlin
m. Maria Vanderbilt
Lewis Chamberlin
m1. Anne Gray
m2. Rachel Brooks
Zilpha Chamberlin

Jesse Chamberlin
m. Effimes
William Chamberlin
m. Elizabeth Duckworth
Mary Chamberlin
m. John Thomson?

129

A MORRIS PRESIDENTIAL RELATIONSHIP

Thomas Morris

Lewis Morris
Elizabeth Almy

Richard Morris

Sarah Morris
Joseph Burdge

Jacob Burdge
Judith Smith

Jacob Burdge Jr.
Miriam Matthews

Oliver Burdge
Jane M. Hemingway

Almira Park Burdge
Franklin Milhous

Hannah Milhous
Francis Athony Nixon

Richard Milhous Nixon
Thelma Catherine "Pat" Ryan

Job Morris
Mary Ansley (of William)

Lydia Morris
Abel Ansley (of Thomas)

Ann Ansley
Wiley Carter

Littleberry Walker Carter
Mary-Ann Diligent Seals

William Archibald Carter
Nina Pratt

James Earl Carter
Bessie Lillian Gordy

James Earl "Jimmy" Carter Jr.
Eleanor Rosalynn Smith

Note: As researched by genealogists, Gary Roberts and Kenneth H. Thomas Jr. and printed in the St. Louis Post Dispatch, November 16, 1980, with minor additions.

Index of Names

Appendix genealogy is not included in index.